Warm regards,
Bill Fisher

YOU ARE NOT A
HOUSE

How to Build Your Real Estate Career
with Passion and Authenticity

BILL FISHER, Ph.D.

The Service-Oriented Marketing Handbook

Trafford
PUBLISHING™

YOU ARE NOT A HOUSE

How to Build Your Real Estate Career with Passion and Authenticity.

FOR INFORMATION,
write to Bill Fisher at wedwrap@comcast.net
OR
Order this book online at www.trafford.com/06-2862
or email orders@trafford.com

This book may be purchased for educational, business or sales promotional use.
Contact Bill Fisher for information.

Note for Librarians: A cataloguing record for this book is available from Library and Archives Canada at www.collectionscanada.ca/amicus/index-e.html

Printed in Victoria, BC, Canada.

ISBN: 978-1-4251-1103-8

10 9 8 7 6 5 4 3 2

CONTENTS

PART ONE

Service-Oriented Marketing

CHAPTER ONE

Success Has No Magical Formula

After I'd been in the real estate business for about two-and-a-half years—which, in this business, used to be a very long time, making me an old pro—a gentleman asked me to interview with him about managing one of his new offices. Understand, the office didn't really exist yet; it was still only a gleam in this guy's eye. But it was, he soon assured me, about to become one of the hottest offices in the state.

So I showed up, notebook in hand, and was ushered into his office. There he sat, minimal hair pomaded to his head, wearing a leisure suit and a pair of mirrored aviator glasses. I held out my hand, which he took curtly, then he sat back and declared, "So, ya wanna make big bucks, eh?"

Honestly, I was stunned. I hadn't been at such a loss for words since some character in a fraternity house whose rush party I was attending with lukewarm interest declared, "So, you gonna tie one on tonight?" What could I say? "Well, no, um. Tomorrow's Wednesday, you know? Classes?"

I simply sat down, dumbfounded, in front of the mirrored aviator glasses, totally unable to see the man's eyes, and said, eventually, "I want the best possible career in real estate."

"Of course," he responded. "Class act."

I asked about the new concept he was so excited about and he swore me to secrecy. "I still gotta keep this under wraps for a while. Can I trust you?"

I assured him that he could. He looked around, as if checking to see if any spies had entered his office while we were talking.

Then: "Don Diego Real Estate," he declared, as if I would fall back in amazement at the cleverness, the ingenuity, the bold creativity behind those four words.

"Yes?" I said, framing it as a question.

"Yes?" he looked at me as if I had nothing between my ears except perhaps the droppings of local seagulls. "It's only going to be the biggest name in real estate...ever!" he said forcefully.

"Because?" I asked quietly.

He paused, collected a deep breath in which, doubtless, he hoped to find the makings of patience. "Because we live in Southern California. Because look," he added, holding up a logo with what appeared to be a smiling unmasked Zorro standing next to the magical words, "Don Diego Real Estate." He gave me a knowing wink. "Get it?" he asked.

"Forgive me," I mumbled.

His voice rose as if he'd reached the higher octane gasoline in his tank. "Listen," he said. "You know Colonel Sanders, right?"

"Right."

"No one sells chicken like Colonel Sanders, right?"

"I suppose," I responded.

"Well, in about a year, no one will be selling houses like Don Diego. He'll become the most recognizable name and face in the business."

"How?" It was bold on my part to ask this question, but I really wanted to know.

"Because he's right!"

"Do you have a marketing plan?" I asked.

"Don't need one. With this name, with this logo, all we need is a few 'For Sale' signs in front of houses, and we're off to the races." He smiled. "You a betting man, Bill?"

"Not really," I admitted.

"Well, I'd be willing to bet you that this will be the strongest real estate company in the area in a year, and you can be the manager of one of the flagship offices."

"All because of this logo," I said, sort of asking, actually.

"All because of this logo," he affirmed.

As it turned out, Don Diego didn't take real estate by storm. Didn't even have its fifteen minutes of fame. It died, not with a bang, but (to paraphrase poet T.S. Eliot) with a whimper.

It takes more than a snappy logo to create something very nearly new in this business. But there is more to the story than that.

A well-designed logo that captures the imagination of those who see it—like a terrific, catchy slogan—can actually do wonders for your business. It is like the code that communicates in one image or in just a few words what you as a real estate professional are all about and how you stand alone in your profession, how no one is quite like you.

Take, for example, the recent slogan used by Safeway—"Ingredients for life"—which communicates (and, equally important, suggests to the subconscious mind) worlds of possible meaning. Allow it to roll around in your brain and, the longer it is there, the more meaning it conveys. It's ingredients *for* life, not *of* life—a very positive statement, suggesting that life will improve, as will health, if you shop at Safeway. Around and around the brain these few words swirl and, like a truly fine wine, their flavor and complexity increase. In short, here's a slogan that works.

Okay, why did an artist's rendering of Colonel Sanders' face work for Kentucky Fried Chicken? For many reasons. We tend to associate great fried chicken with Southern cooking, and a traditional, portly "colonel" seems a great candidate for the developer of a wonderful recipe. His presence on the company sign, in the advertising and on the carton of food also adds a personal feeling—as if here is someone who is willing to stake his reputation on our enjoyment of a box of fried chicken. Here, in short, is a logo that works.

What, then, could be said for an artist's rendering of a smiling "Don Diego"? What, for starters, does Don Diego's obvious counterpart, Zorro, something of an early California Robin Hood, have to do with real estate? In what way does his image suggest that this company is going to provide us with a good experience when we buy or sell real estate? How does his smiling face, his arm confidently draped over a 'For Sale' sign, his sturdy posture encapsulate what we might want buyers and sellers to know about the way our real estate company does business and how it will benefit them?

Obviously, it does none of these things. My acquaintance, who was so certain he had discovered the Next Big Thing in Southern California real estate, had committed what is probably the most common error in real estate marketing.

You see, there is a single underlying principle that almost every one of us has violated at some point in our career—probably many times—and that my marketing colleagues and I have learned to follow from our combined years of study and experience....

The central error most people commit is thinking from the vantage point of their own professional needs, rather than from the vantage point of their client's and prospective client's personal needs.

Thus, the marketing program presented in this book, which we have come to call service-oriented marketing, serves clients' and prospective clients' needs **first**...not our own. But by doing so— believe me—it serves our own needs better than any other possible marketing program.

A paradox? Perhaps. But you will not be able to wrap your mind around service-oriented marketing, nor will you be able to get the full benefits it has to offer, until you begin to understand this paradox.

What are our own needs? We want the phone to ring. We want to sit down with potential clients in our conference room. We want to list houses. We want to sell houses. We want to make a living. I mean, please!

But what do our clients and potential clients need and want? They want to work with someone who is knowledgeable, trustworthy, energetic. They want someone who is at least somewhat like-minded, someone who can truly hear them and act on their requests and help to translate their dreams into reality, someone who will be an invaluable coach for the team that gets their home sold and their next home purchase closed—without unexpected profit losses, without legal hassles, without pain and gnashing of teeth, without threats involving bizarre martial arts and emotional torture, etc., etc.

Throughout this book, I will bring a series of extremely important— and traditionally overlooked—principles to your attention. Therefore:

Service-Oriented Marketing Principle #1:
Design all your marketing and prospecting with your clients' needs in mind. Not your own needs.

Before you do anything, see it through the eyes of people who want to sell their home and/or buy another home. That is their aim, and they are more sophisticated today than ever before. Their increased awareness of all that goes into the buying and selling of a home has convinced them they need professional assistance. And—hopefully—your marketing program has all but convinced them you're the one they want to work with.

Maybe seeing things through the eyes of your clients seems a bit obvious to you, but I promise: it's not. Name other business professionals, for example, who think they should advertise to potential clients by citing the fact that they are members of the Hundred Million Dollar Golden Jubilee Club (or whatever designation your company comes up with for its top salespeople)?

I can think of one. McDonalds. "One hundred billion burgers sold." But even they dropped that advertising campaign. (They probably ran out of room on their marquees for the lengthy numbers.)

You are not a hamburger.

You are a human being who offers her or his accumulated knowledge, experience, intuition, intelligence, energy and wit to help certain people find precisely the house that will serve them, at the best possible price, with the best possible terms. Again, this is no small task. Not the sort of task that comes down the conveyer belt like precisely-cooked meat patties, waiting for the cookie-cutter hamburger buns. Not the sort of task that the Internet will ever handle more effectively than a great real estate professional. The sort of task, instead, that requires precisely your abilities.

What your prospective clients need to know is who you are, how you work, what you "promise" their experience will consist of if they work with you. ("Promise," as we will soon see, is an important word in the world of marketing.)

And that raises another problem. When we write classified advertisements trying to get people to call and ask questions about advertised houses, the whole point is to get the telephone to ring. We write coy and catchy descriptions of a home, leaving out key information so that people will have questions and call to ask them.

But when we advertise ourselves or develop a personal marketing campaign to bring in a steady flow of clients over time and create a gold mine of a target market, all too often the question we ask about the advertisement or newsletter or whatever marketing piece we send out is: "How many telephone calls did it bring in?"

You are not a house.

Nor are your potential clients.

Hence the title of this book. You do not motivate people to become your clients by publishing advertisements that call you a Comfy Charmer. In fact, you can't convincingly tell people how they should think about you. You can't, for example, say you are as honest as the day is long. That's as credible as a crocodile's tears.

At the same time, your client is likewise not a house. He or she is not a three bdrm w/FR and view. Not table 34 in a restaurant. Not bed 18 in the hospital (nor is he or she "the angiogram" in #18). And not a jerk, not a commission check, not even a "prospect." She or he is a human with a serious set of needs, wishes, problems and possible solutions…and THAT is what (or rather whom) you should be addressing.

There have been so many ways of making it difficult to work with people. Let's leave that behind once and for all. Let's work with the human being with his and her own needs and wishes, rather than armwrestling with that "live one" we hope to wangle a commission check out of. And let's work to develop a steady stream of human beings with whom we can work effectively and profitably.

There is, as we shall see, so very much that we can do to build a great clientele, a constant flow of transactions, a stream of interesting and simpatico clients, and a truly rich and successful career in this business.

Let's begin!

CHAPTER TWO

A Change Of Perspective And Attitude

It turns out that bringing in a steady stream of great clients is no easy task. In fact, if you're not thinking from the perspective of their needs, you could face a huge amount of frustration.

Consider the following facts:

▶ 1. Americans, on average, move once every five to seven years. Some of them rent. Some of them live with their mothers. Some of them sell their home and move to a new one.

Okay—let's say you walk up and down the streets of your city shouting, "Is anyone thinking of buying or selling a home?" Obviously, an astonishingly small number of those who hear your desperate voice will, at that moment, be thinking of buying or selling a home. And a minuscule number will actually admit it. I mean, why should they admit it to you?

If you're trying to find a client or two and do some business, this can be a problem. And the problem gets worse. (But things also do get better, as you will see time and again in this book.)

▶ 2. "Sellers take an average of 9.3 months from the time they begin actively thinking about a sale until the close date," according to an extensive recent survey and study conducted by Hebert Research for House Values, Inc. (I'm quoting a *Realtor® Magazine Online* article by Blanche Evans here.) But once they decide to sell, they "take only one day to select a real estate practitioner."

In other words, the window of opportunity for a real estate professional is astonishingly small. It's not inappropriate to say that you have roughly one day in the lengthy cycle of someone's decision to sell their home to call through their window: "Hey! Need some help selling this place?" Kind of like trying to sell life insurance to a cicada, a singing insect that comes around with his family and friends for only a few weeks once every thirteen years.

What about buyers? The distance from first contemplating the purchase of a home to actually completing the deal is, on the average, 16.7 months—and they "select their real estate practitioner within just one to three days."

So if you're wandering around the neighborhood, asking if anyone is thinking of buying or selling a home, your chances of finding a really good potential client are slim. You surely will at some point—just as you would very likely bring down an edible Canada Goose or other migrating fowl eventually by standing out in your yard each morning and shooting a shotgun blindly into the air—but there has to be a better way!

And there is. But I digress.

▶ 3. When people decide to buy and/or sell a house, you can't tell it just by looking at them. Their skin and hair don't turn a slightly different color. They don't wear an odd house-seller's expression on their faces. They don't put on a tee shirt that says, "I need a real estate professional pronto." There is no way to tell them from others who have no intention whatsoever of moving to a new home.

Perhaps you begin to understand why some people who try to make a living in real estate seem to age so quickly. The phone rings and they mutter odd, incoherent phrases under their breath. "Two o'clock, or would three be better for you?" "My name is Joe Doakes. Yours?" Mutter mutter. "Oh, that home is a real cream puff!" Things like that—before they even pick up the phone.

And that's only one side of the story. Let's say you find yourself talking to some people who called up to ask about that "Comfy Charmer" your office manager is advertising in the classified ads. They ask you about the home and suddenly your job is to throw up body blocks and head fakes, changing the subject at every opportunity from the advertised house to the carefully-disguised fact that you want to make an appointment to meet with them in your office and to nail them to a seat, win them over, have their tennis shoes bronzed, call them clients, sell them something.

Step one in this little drama, therefore, is to get over a small mountain of mutual skepticism and distrust. And again…there has to be a better way.

And again, in most cases there is!

What we have here, in this book—and I hasten to add that I don't own a pair of mirrored aviator glasses, or even a leisure suit, or the rights to a snappy new logo—what we have here is a dramatically new way of marketing yourself and building a successful, gratifying career in real estate.

It is not, however, a lot of spicy, never-before-seen, just-add-water-and-mix material, as you'll quickly realize.

All too many marketing programs for real estate and mortgage professionals over the years have sounded too much like the magic promised by get-rich-quick schemes in very old comic books…"Utter the thirteen Magic Power Words and you'll have clients totally under your control." It probably won't surprise you to learn there are no such thirteen words, nor magic Internet advertising machines, nor power handshakes that make people need to buy from no one but you. It's still tempting, admittedly. But the path to a wonderful career in real estate has very few short cuts (though it has multiple maddening potential detours). I suppose, in truth, that the greatest short cut is knowing what works and what doesn't, so you don't waste your time, energy and money on ineffectual nonsense. That and keeping your eye on the ball—remembering Principle #1—thinking from the vantage point of your clients and potential clients.

The fact is, this book weaves together principles and activities that will be, for the most part, at least somewhat familiar to most readers. Staying in touch with past clients, after all, isn't a radical idea (though a phenomenally small percentage of real estate professionals do so). Nor is writing effective classified ads. Nor is sending out an engaging and informative newsletter every month. Nor are many of the remaining ideas detailed in this book.

What's new here is the way it all comes together—and the successful and fulfilling experience it brings. And what's new rests on a foundation of a clearer understanding of how your own attitude toward your business and your clients determines the quantity and quality of your transactions. What's also new is that you become immune to the traps that catch you up in the kind of burn-out that ends so many promising careers early. Further, you realize that the only real boundaries on your success are created by your own expectations, fears and uncertainties. And the marketing you do, as you will discover, aligns itself with who you are—not with some manipulative Mr. or Ms. Selling Machine that you are convinced you must become—and personal marketing comes as naturally to you as telling your favorite joke or helping a friend in need.

Your Attitude Will Determine
The Quality Of Your Business Experience.

Early on in my real estate career, I made a friend who was extremely intelligent, who undoubtedly had an extraordinarily high IQ, but who was strangely lacking in common street smarts and in what has recently come to be called emotional intelligence. Though a very nice guy, he habitually referred to his clients as "assholes." (Sorry if that offends you—and it should—but it's the actual word he used…constantly.)

Guess what? He was right. They were. To a man and woman, they were, undeniably, assholes. And unlike my friend, I don't use that word lightly or easily.

With his restless intelligence, my friend made matters even worse, writing up deals that were bound and determined to explode like trick cigars in everyone's faces—with multiple unnecessary contingencies, carpet allowances, appliance allowances, cleaning charges, and on and on. He was miserably unhappy…but it didn't take a degree in psychology to understand why.

For rather similar reasons, a very intelligent CPA who worked in my office was constantly full of frustrations. He chased after huge and complex transactions, many of them involving multiple commercial real estate projects. Whenever I wandered past his desk and asked how he was doing, he responded, "Well, I'm just trying to put something together here." Or "Just tryin' to make a buck." And that was exactly what he was doing—trying, always. It may seem an innocent response on his part, but he almost never moved past the word, "trying," to an actual deal. Instead of putting something together, he was always trying to do so.

Notice that these are self-fulfilling prophecies. Both of these fine men needed to do some work on their sense of what was possible for them. With these attitudes, they were fated to look at the successes of others and wonder why the others had all the luck and they didn't. The answer to that question, of course, is that it isn't luck that brings you what you experience. More than anything else, it's the distorting lens of your own emotional attitude—and the magical fact, which I observed countless times as the manager of a real estate office, is that people experience what they expect to experience. You expect asshole; you get asshole. You very nearly become a magnet that attracts them to your phone, your open houses, your office hours.

Now, it's not very helpful to simply tell such a person, "Change your attitude, for heaven's sake." We'll do that in this book, inevitably—but in such a way that changing your attitude comes to make all the sense in the world.

What we can say, though—and we'll repeat this often—is:

Service-Oriented Marketing Principle #2:
Know Thyself.

The more you can learn about your own expectations and your own sense of who you are, the better-equipped you will be to market yourself to people with whom you work well, people who reflect the best in you, instead of people who amplify your weaknesses.

Avoiding The Shooting Star Traps:

Unfortunately, many real estate companies value their agents primarily, if not solely, for the volume of business they're doing right now. There is far too little attention paid to the lasting, dependable, successful careers that can be encouraged and nourished by good office and sales managers.

As a consequence, the real estate field has traditionally rewarded only their top-dollar-volume salespeople...with praise, plaques, statues, award ceremonies and other ephemeral nonsense. The first company I worked for, then a Southern California giant, rewarded its top salespeople at the end of one summer with a trip to Catalina in perhaps the slowest and most unstable (and, doubtless, cheapest) boat ever to make the journey. I made a lasting friend when I cleaned up the contents of her stomach which she had emptied on herself as we made our merry way over the endless huge swells heading home after a total of three memory-soaked hours in Avalon. All of which made me very leery of accepting any further awards from my company for my salesmanship.

Earlier on, though, when I received my first "Quota Buster" plaque (signifying that I'd taken two listings, made one sale of another agent's listing, and had one of my listings sell, all in one month, sports fans!), I telephoned my father with the exciting news. He listened impatiently, then asked, "Can you eat the plaque?"

I was crushed, of course, but the question served me very well over the years—sort of a helpful way of saying, "Keep your eyes on the ball, boy." Keep your eyes on the development of your career…and the quality of the food on your dinner table.

Sadly, we salespeople have too often been sucked into the momentum of this top-salesman approach, coming to believe that it's more important to "amp up" the amount of business we're doing than it is (a) to create and achieve goals that support the life we want to live and (b) to live a balanced and satisfying life. It's not more important. It's anything *but* more important.

Still, management all too often helps turn its agents into burn-outs. Several real estate companies have been well known for their "Chinese army" approach to the business, enticing as many new agents as possible into their offices, then pressuring them to produce as many deals as possible until they virtually die under the weight of the demand to bring in more and more deals. Finally, they move on to another way of making a living. And for the companies, it's "good riddance" to agents who've brought in most of the deals they can easily and quickly bring in from friends, family and other contacts.

This is absurd. Not only does it hurt many people, it also hurts the companies that perpetrate such thoughtless policies. It costs a great deal more to keep filling desks with new agents than it does to have those desks occupied by people who know what they want and who continue to reach their goals, even if they're not setting the world on fire with their sales volume. Training new agents is in every way a very expensive process. Maintaining positive office morale and building company identity is incredibly difficult if there is a high turnover.

Pressure from management and from your peers to perform wonders makes it difficult to avoid the shooting star traps. It is helpful to work with management and other salespeople who understand that you are developing a career that will last and support your life goals—even more helpful if they are doing the same thing. But the single most important thing to do, and we will work on this in coming chapters, is to know who you are, what you want, and what your ideal target market looks like—then to market yourself to those people effectively, never forgetting to lay the groundwork for tomorrow's transactions while prospecting for those of today.

Service-Oriented Marketing Principle #3:
Always keep the bigger, whole-career picture in mind, not just short-term concerns.

Expanding and clarifying your expectations of what you can and will get from your marketing efforts is central to a rich and fulfilling career in real estate.

In short, marketing is about ever so much more than just getting some unknown person to call you on the phone so you can talk him or her into the office for an appointment. It is not a manipulative battle—especially now that most clients are far more sophisticated than they used to be. Your marketing, when all is said and done, is the way you let the right people know who you are and why they should call on you when they need the professional assistance that you can give them so well. In successful marketing, you begin to build relationships of trust, developing a target market made up of people who feel they know you, even though you may not yet know them.

You want your marketing to bring you "warm" and even "hot" clients who are relatively pre-sold on you, not skeptical strangers whose first anxious priority is to stay out of your manipulative clutches. You want people who share many of your likes and dislikes, people to whom you can relate deeply and well (and vice versa), people whom you can serve...rather than battle. And you want a constant flow of such people and, as a result, a constant income stream and sense of satisfaction in your work.

You want your marketing to bring precisely these people into your life. You want—and expect—nothing less from your marketing. A transaction with clients who neither like nor trust you all too often ends with bad feelings all around and, though you may still get a commission from the deal, you will pay for it over and over again as these clients spread their negative version of who you are to everyone who will listen.

What is a "warm" client? It's someone who already knows who you are and has a good feeling about working with you. A "hot" client? That's the person who calls you up and says, "Hey, I've been reading your newsletter for months and it's great! When can you come over and list my house?"

You want a marketing program that, insofar as is possible, brings you "warm" and "hot" clients. They are extremely valuable to the quality of your work experience, and invaluable to the quality of your overall career.

Service-Oriented Marketing Principle #4:
A "warm" client is far more likely to result in a good transaction, which will bring in similar "warm" clients in the future.

Marketing stops being an odd, alien activity when it is simply the way you do your business—staying in touch with people who matter to you, helping people at the drop of a hat, sharing the benefit of your accumulated knowledge, giving back to the community that supports you. And yes, that isn't just how you do your business; it's how you live a truly rich and healthy life.

We're talking about a way of life, you see, not just a lead-generating system. We're talking about creating a real estate career that maximizes all you uniquely bring to it, leaves you time and energy for other activities that are crucial to your personal growth and well-being, and allows you to stay in integrity with your highest ideals and deepest pleasures.

CHAPTER THREE
Running With The Expectation Of Success

"My ideal athlete was first and foremost a human being who ran his sport and did not allow it to run him." –Roger Bannister

A little over fifty years ago, as I am writing these words, Roger Bannister became the first human being ever officially to run the mile in less than four minutes. Now, four minutes may seem, in the great scheme of things, a rather arbitrary number, but it's well worth remembering that people generally assumed that no human being could run a four-minute mile until about 1950 (though there were a few unofficial reports of such a feat before Bannister broke the barrier). And even then, most were skeptical.

Since then, of course, hundreds if not thousands of runners have completed the mile run in less than four minutes. The world record has been broken again and again, as runners continue to slice seconds and fractions of seconds off of the former record time.

It's almost as if one day everyone assumed it couldn't be done, the next day it was done, and in the days following more and more runners repeated the deed, often improving on it. Where did these guys come from? (I say "guys," by the way, since a woman hasn't beaten the 4-minute mile time—yet.)

For me, the phenomenon of moving from no one running the mile in less than four minutes to a growing army of 4-minute milers is astonishing. It's like something invented for an old episode of *Twilight Zone*. I find myself wondering if an alien force somehow infected the human race, elevating the possibilities for runners with imported supernatural powers.

But no. It wasn't an infusion of alien energies. It wasn't magic. It wasn't even the *Twilight Zone*. It was precisely what makes us become more than we were and do more than we ever thought possible for ourselves.

Bannister, who was a medical student at the time and went on to enjoy a brilliant career as a neurologist, approached his running with great modesty. He describes his early experiences of running with profound emotion and near-mysticism: "The earth seemed almost to move with me. I was running now, and a fresh rhythm entered my body. No longer conscious of my movement I discovered a new unity with nature. I had found a new source of power and beauty, a source I never dreamt existed."

Was Bannister intrinsically the best runner on earth? Not as he tells it. "I am sure that I was not a better runner than the others, in the sense of having more innate ability." He ran in his youth because he loved it and because, given how intensely shy he was, it gave him acceptance among his peers in school.

What, then, transformed a young man, wiry, gentle, light of frame, into the first runner to beat the four minute mark? Here the story becomes very intriguing and, for the purposes of this book, extremely relevant.

To put it as simply as possible, he gathered together all that was known about running—the physiology, the psychology of the runner, the best equipment to use—and put that together with his awareness of the best training program (for him, not necessarily for others), and then trained in his own unique fashion in such a way that his ability, his strength and endurance would all peak at the time of an important race. To that, I would add an all-important factor: Bannister *expected* to beat the four-minute mark—expected, at the very least, that if he wasn't the first to do so, someone would do it soon.

> *"Was it possible for a man to run a mile in four minutes? To me the answer was obvious. Of course, as a result of more competition and better training, men would gradually run miles in faster and faster times, until four minutes was reached. Nor would the progress stop there. For an improvement that cannot go on indefinitely there must be a limit. But rather as the tortoise in the mathematical problem, based on Æsop's fable, is never caught by the hare running at twice the speed, so the limit in miling would never be reached, although the margin by which the record was broken would continually diminish."*

I believe that, if we are to achieve something, we must somehow believe it to be possible. And that once we gain such a belief, we have the expectation that everything we do to achieve our goal will get us a bit closer to it…and the expectation that one day we'll get there.

This is not to say that we are limited to achieving only what we believe is possible for us. It is to say that our sense of the possible and our expectation of reaching it points us in the right direction, and the results may even exceed our wildest expectations. "If we aim at a star," Bannister writes, "we may occasionally reach a height normally beyond us."

Service-Oriented Marketing Principle #5: Always expect the best for your clients and from your clients, and also for yourself and from yourself.

The most important element in Bannister's success, I think, was his sense of what is possible and his expectation of achieving it. But there is a very important caveat here.

Roger Bannister ran his record-breaking mile while a medical student. He had a full life, many friends, many interests—and he had a career planned beyond his running. He was not obsessed with his sport. He didn't, as he says, let his running run his life.

And this is true and crucial for other professions as well.

This book now in your hands spells out a new way of looking at and creating your own personal marketing program and, indeed your entire career and life, one that you should customize just as Bannister customized his own training program. It is designed especially for real estate professionals, though many in other sales positions—and in very different businesses—will benefit greatly from the principles and nuts-and-bolts steps outlined in this book. Everyone studying these marketing techniques should adapt them to her and his own personality, character, goals, interests, passions, and very way of being in the world.

One of the things we will do, in spite of our focus on Roger Bannister's amazing feat, is to move away from the tired idea of being the winner, the champion, the superstar in the sales business. Though Bannister was, for a brief time, something of a superstar, that wasn't his focus. He wanted to run, and to run competitively, and then to become a doctor, never letting fame get in his way.

And he made certain, every step of the way, that he lived as balanced a life as possible, always retaining a sense of who he was, what he loved to do, and all that he wanted in his life.

Service-Oriented Marketing Principle #6:
You must love and enjoy what you are doing, and make sure you have time for all that you love in your life.

You get to be the one who is in charge of your life, and your real estate career must support the entirety of your life—your family, your friendships, your loves, your hobbies, your community work, your social and spiritual endeavors. Your career doesn't get to run your life. You are not a house.

It's simple. If you don't follow this principle, you may become something of a superstar, but in reality you will only be a comet, trailing dust and eventually burning out. There is no reason ever that this should happen to you. So we'll keep in mind, throughout this book, the ways that we can nurture ourselves, our lives and the lives of those who matter the most to us.

Those nurturing endeavors, and the fun and satisfaction they bring, are the main reasons we work as hard as we do, after all.

The difference, if you use the principles and take the practical steps outlined here, is that fun and satisfaction will become built-in components of your work style.

CHAPTER FOUR
How This Book Came To Be

About nineteen years ago, a fellow named Rand Fleischman called me. I was at that precise moment sitting at my computer in my home office in Valley Center, California, looking lazily out of my window at the face of Mount Palomar, warming my mental engines to the task of writing my next newsletter.

Rand had developed a company that provided real estate brokers with weekly copy for columns in local newspapers. He had an independent contractor or two writing the columns, a salesman out finding clients, and his part of the job was to interface with the local newspaper, making sure the column appeared correctly and attractively in the newspaper—no small task.

Though his clients were happy with the results, many of them wondered if he had a monthly newsletter that they might buy. So Rand decided to develop one.

He studied the entire field, looking at all the real estate prospecting newsletters available, bringing to bear his considerable experience of marketing and psychology—and he decided that the newsletter I was producing with my friend and partner Mike Eggers (who did the formatting and design) was the best in the field. So he called me. He didn't expect me to work for him. He was, after all, about to market a newsletter that would compete with mine, and he assumed I'd want no part of competing with myself.

He was wrong.

I liked this guy. He was warm, straightforward, extremely knowledgeable, and knew what he wanted. And besides, he did a great job of buttering up my ego.

I told him I'd love to help develop and then write a prospecting letter with him. Noticing that he was flabbergasted, I asked a simple pair of questions: "How many real estate agents do you suppose there are in just the state of California alone? And how many of them do you need to sign up for your newsletter before it begins to make you a meaningful profit?"

He was silent for a moment. "I just never in the world thought you'd say 'yes,'" he admitted. And thus began a working relationship that has expanded exponentially over the years, becoming an extremely close friendship in time. Rand's wife, Jill, who was then working as a therapist, joined us later, bringing extraordinary people skills to the business. Our relationship took a quantum leap the day she called me and, hearing a bit of despair in my voice, asked what was wrong. And I, for some reason, told her—let it all tumble out. My Dad had Alzheimer's Disease, my Mom was suffering from the miserable effects of several strokes—couldn't talk, couldn't dial a phone, couldn't make sense of a tragically altered world. And I was their primary caretaker, receiving about eight calls a day from my father, who was filled constantly with paranoid delusions.

Jill was so extraordinarily present to me, gentle and caring, that I realized this would be a friend of inestimable value. Rand, though quieter in his counsel, was, at the very least, equally valuable to me, and they both helped me through one of the hardest times in my life.

As our relationship developed, we found we all had a deep curiosity about—indeed, a passion for—effective marketing. Rand had, among other things, worked as Head of Membership for the Los Angeles County Art Museum, and had had a big taste of the difficulties inherent to direct mailing campaigns. He also holds a Master's Degree in counseling. I'd been a real estate professional and broker-owner of a medium-sized office in southern Orange County; I'd been writing and marketing real estate prospecting newsletters since 1980; and my background included a Ph.D. in medieval English literature (to be honest with you, such a degree isn't absolutely necessary in real estate practice, but it's always gotten a good laugh when I'm being introduced as a participant in a panel of speakers whose other experts all have a Ph.D. in economics), and a fair amount of teaching. And Jill's background and experience in therapy and the performing arts added further to the diversity of experience and expertise that went into the creation of our real estate marketing products and the philosophy behind them.

It's a pleasing success story. Plenty of chicken soup here.

We know from experience that our products work, that they truly support real estate and mortgage professionals who are passionate about using and benefiting from them. Over the years, we developed new products, opened our marketing area further and further, and always—at our meetings, in our emails, in telephone conversations—we expanded and sharpened our idea of why these products worked and what philosophy of marketing and sales they represented.

It has been an exciting, long-term conversation. Thankfully, we all know and trust each other well enough to be able to say, "That's ridiculous," whenever in fact it is. Equally important, when we bounce ideas off of one another it often feels like sparks are flying among fireworks. Invariably, a conversation about a question or idea develops into something worthy of further discussion and thought.

It occurred to us that we needed to write a lengthy brochure because our approach to marketing is quite different from the tired old Direct Response methods used exclusively for about a century in real estate. (Understand that our approach doesn't eliminate the benefits of Direct Response marketing; instead, it amps up what you can expect from *all* your marketing efforts.)

Here's the problem we kept running into. A client, having sent out perhaps two monthly newsletters, would call and say the program wasn't working for him. He hadn't had one listing, one sale or even one call as a result of sending those newsletters out. We felt we needed a brochure that explained the difference between marketing for one listing or sale vs. marketing for a career, marketing a house vs. marketing yourself. We also needed to provide data showing that homebuyers and homesellers take, on average, about a year to get from the first "Honey-I've-been-thinking" to actually buying their first home or selling their existing home and buying another. And as we talked about what we wanted to include in our brochure, it kept expanding until it became a book.

As you can probably tell, this book wouldn't exist if I hadn't had a long-term working relationship with Rand and Jill. Their ideas and creativity can be found in every page (though you can place all the blame on me if you find a page or two that you disagree with.)

And here are two of several principles that can be drawn from this experience:

Service-Oriented Marketing Principle #7:
Learn all you can from those among your fellow associates at work who offer support, stimulate your mind, and model the ways of doing business that you wish to emulate.

This turns out to be incredibly important. Run your ideas up the flagpole and see if anyone salutes. Don't be intimidated if people react to your plans as "unorthodox" and "probably unworkable." But don't place yourself in a position where you are constantly reinventing the proverbial wheel.

It is crucial to be yourself in this business, and crucial not to fall into the trap of copying some sales guru. At the same time, though, your progress up the path toward success will be greatly accelerated if you surround yourself with people who have already made it up some of the paths you're working on. They will encourage you, show you what worked for them, and pick you up when you stumble. And it's important to avoid feeling alone.

Service-Oriented Marketing Principle #8:
Do not limit your friendships to your own office or company, and do not let the misleading idea that someone is your "competition" keep you from creating beneficial relationships with such people.

I pointed out to Rand that there are several hundred thousand people in California alone with real estate licenses, and that neither of us needed more than a few hundred of those people as clients in order for our marketing businesses to thrive.

One result of this insight: We astonish many people who call to inquire about our products and services because we always suggest that they study all newsletters being provided by other companies as closely as possible. "Why would you want us to do that?" they ask, arguing that, "those people are your competition." The fact is, if someone likes another company's services better than ours, he or she should work with the other company.

There's another underlying principle here. It works far better if you approach your business assuming you don't really have any "competition." You are unique. No one offers quite what you offer. You are precisely the right person for a specific, large sector of the marketplace.

Here are two results of such thinking. First, your so-called competition becomes, more correctly, colleagues from whom you can learn and—crucially—the workforce that will help sell your listings. It is worth cultivating good relationships with these people.

Second, if you construct your personal marketing program with your "competition" in mind—if you set out to "beat the competition" with your marketing program—you will frame most of what you do in the same terms used by others. Your uniqueness and originality will fall by the wayside. Instead of bringing something very new and effective to your marketing, you will almost certainly get stuck in an effort to do what everyone else is doing, only better. (See Part 7: A New Framework, for a further discussion of opening innovation by closing our tired, outmoded assumptions about competition.)

Why make sure people have seen other products before signing up with our program, then?

My colleagues and I believe—and have very often been told—that ours are the best personal marketing products on the market...but we know that the products and services aren't for everyone. There are certain personality types that our newsletters and other products just won't represent very well at all. And it's crucial that everyone who uses our products feel at home with them. (One long-term client, a mortgage professional, assured me that our *Lender Letter* was a perfect fit for her because I write and think the way she does. This isn't always necessary, but clients should feel they can stand proudly behind the newsletters and other materials they send out.)

Bottom line: You are working in a universe of your own in real estate. You'll be precisely the right agent for certain people, but not for all people. And you will actually benefit by seeking to do business with the first group, and leaving the second group to your real estate colleagues.

And that defines yet another exceedingly important principle:

Service-Oriented Marketing Principle #9:
You, as a real estate professional, are not the right person for every potential client in the known universe.

One of the most personally-empowering things you can do is to "fire" a client when it becomes clear that you are not going to work well together. After all, fireworks are the likely result here...nasty ones that burn your career in the future as disgruntled clients spread negative stories about you.

You see, it's not just a matter of your personal happiness and the level of your blood pressure. Your business will work far, far better if you only seek out clients with whom you can work well, people who will trust you and appreciate what you have to offer. These are the people who will multiply the effects of your marketing by telling friends, family and business associates good things about you. Their help as you develop your career is more valuable than an effective billboard on the main street of your city or town.

CHAPTER FIVE

A Very Brief History Of Real Estate Marketing

O ne of the reasons it doesn't take long to provide a history of the marketing techniques used in real estate is that there just haven't been very many, and most of them have been extremely simple—as simple as sitting down by a little body of water and throwing in your hook and line, hoping that some unlucky fish might nibble at some point.

Consider: Joe Doakes, Realtor®

Let's imagine it's about 1965. Joe Doakes, retired U.S. Army Master Sergeant, got his real estate license in 1963 and went to work in a small office whose manager said, "There's your desk, there's your phone, good luck"—a training program that was undeniably elegant in its brevity.

Joe sat down and went to work. He brought in the newspaper every morning, along with a huge thermos of coffee capable of killing lesser mortals, sat down with his feet up on his desk, his telephone near at hand, and read the paper and drank the coffee. Occasionally, some poor soul called the office to ask about a home for sale. They'd either seen a 'For Sale' sign in front of the house and written down the office telephone number, or they'd read a classified ad that described the property in evasive language. ("Total cream puff, 1800sf, huge mbr, seller anxious, make offer.")

"Doakes Reelity," Joe would intone if the phone rang, for he now owned his own small office—a weathered mobile home by the railroad track with a sign that shouted from his window, "We Need Listings." (Note, too, that he had taken on the popular mispronunciation of "realty." The word is correctly pronounced "Ree-uhl-tee," not "Ree-li-tee.")

"Hello," a voice would say uncertainly. "Can you tell me about this 'total cream puff' you're advertising?"

"Who am I speaking with?" Joe would ask.

"Does it matter?"

"Well," Joe would explain, using the same line he'd used hundreds of times, "our sellers don't want us giving our information to people who aren't truly interested in their home. You never can tell these days, you know? What with robbings and murders and whatnot."

"My name is Jean Chewsky," the voice said softly. "Can you tell me about this house?"

"What would you like to know?" Joe would ask, sounding oddly like the fox in the Æsop's fable about the bird with the bread in its mouth.

From here forward, Joe would do all he could to tell Jean Chewsky as little as he could about the house in question. Instead, he would continually say, "I'd be more than happy to show you this beautiful home at your convenience. Would you prefer one o'clock this afternoon, or would three o'clock work better for you?"

Finally, in exasperation, Jean Chewsky said, "Three o'clock will be fine. Where shall I meet you?"

And Joe, smacking his lips slightly, declared, "Why, here at my office. I'll have a cup of coffee waiting for you."

The whole point of this charade, of course, was to get a potential client into the office. Once in the office, Joe could get some idea of what she was truly looking for; could get vital data like income, phone number, current address; could show her a few houses, starting with his own listings, whether or not they met Jean's stated needs. ("Now this particular house doesn't match what you've told me exactly, but I think you'll find it has a tremendous number of unusually nice features.")

But there are two immediate problems with this approach.

First, notice that Joe and Jean Chewsky are at odds from the get-go. This is not a matter of one person coming with a set of needs to a seasoned professional whom she trusts. It is more a matter of constantly having to beat back this old Master Sergeant, as if he kept holding her under water precisely when she needed to come up for air. It is true that she wants to buy a home and he wants to sell her one, but it is not true that his first aim is to find her the home that truly meets her needs and fulfills her dreams. He simply wants to make a sale, and he believes that he has to apply some verbal arm-twisting to do so.

So they aren't at all on the same sheet of music. Jean will probably buy a home in spite of Joe Doakes, not because of his help, and they may even reach the point where they nearly like and perhaps trust one another. But it all comes down to this simple matter: Joe can make the appointments and open the lock boxes. Without him, she most likely couldn't get into the houses she wants to see. (And she finds out what she wants to see—this being, remember, 1965—because Joe sends her home with the prior week's multiple listing book after their first meeting. This has changed, of course, because all that data is now readily available on the Internet.)

Joe certainly doesn't qualify as the coach who helps Jean fulfill some lifelong dreams and wishes. Theirs is an awkward, strained relationship from the start.

Second, therefore: When the eventual purchase transaction does close, Jean is very unlikely to suggest Joe's name to friends and associates who are looking for a home. So Joe's business will forever seem to him a matter of luck—sitting by the telephone and sitting in open houses, waiting for someone to wander his way, hoping the person won't be too much of a creep.

Marketing Takes A Step Forward

Let's say it's 1978 now, and the world of real estate is abuzz with a new marketing technique called "farming." Apparently developed by the head of a real estate training school—or so he claimed—named John Lumbleau, a big man with a big ego and a room-filling voice. "Farming" replaced "fishing" to some degree.

"Farming" was a proactive approach to marketing yourself, not just a reactive way of responding to people who called on ads and visited open houses. You picked a residential area, claimed it as your own, and started working it—nurturing it, sowing your marketing materials, constantly asking for (rather than just waiting for) a bumper crop of listings. "Remember," John Lumbleau's voice would boom out, "always to ask for the order. Otherwise, you're not likely to get it."

"Farmers" paid for their clientele with shoe leather. They walked the streets of their chosen neighborhood, stopping at each house, knocking on the door, perhaps handing out something to the person who answered the door (a pad to be used for grocery lists, a cheap calendar, a business card), and they would crank up a tired smile and repeat their sales mantra, again and again, "Hi, I'm Davey Eggleston with Doowop Realtors. Are you, or is anyone you know, thinking of buying or selling real estate anytime soon?"

Lo and behold, now and again someone would say, "Yes. Why, my Uncle Harlance is thinking of moving here from Horse's Breath, Alabama." And the real estate agent/farmer had the potential makings, weak though they might be, of a future deal.

The king of the early farmers was a young lad named Tommy Hopkins. (At this point, for some reason—perhaps to make themselves appear extra user-friendly—the successful real estate trainers all had names like Tommy, Danny, and Bobbie. Tommy, after his early farming success, became one of the most famous of these sales trainers, and remains one of the most famous to this day.) Tommy Hopkins had no suit of clothes when he started in the business, so he put on his high school band uniform and started walking his farm area.

He made a crucial discovery. If you stop and talk to people, and if you see them fairly often, you develop relationships that not only turn into future business, but also turn into *high quality* future business. He also discovered that you have to keep on keeping on. You can develop good rapport with people but you need to continue to show up and remind those people of your existence, so that when the time comes for them to buy, sell or refinance, you'll still be the person they think of. You can't count on two door-knockings, two newsletters, two favorable impressions to bring you business. You have to stay at it, make it a part of your life.

He didn't take these discoveries quite as far as he might have, and the reason may have been that he was infected with the "champion" bug. As people in the phenomenal real estate market of the late 1970s began to make a lot of money—before the recession hit—real estate and mortgage professionals, whose primary prior experience of greatness may indeed have been playing trombone in the school band, became intoxicated with just how rich they could become, and the possibility that their new-found wealth would also bring respect, fame, and happiness. (I remember one day being interrupted as I worked at my desk by an office-mate named Doris, who asked, in her deep Southern accent, "Beeull, do y'all feel like y'all wasted yer entire life before ya got into real estate?" "No," I responded, but she didn't hear me.)

Tommy took to the road, offering up seminars on becoming a real estate champion, and in the process he became as much a real estate evangelist as he was a superb sales trainer. There is nothing wrong with evangelizing, of course—except that it placed the emphasis on becoming a (generally momentary) champion rather than on having a great life and career. Further, what he was selling his adoring students was his own way of doing business, his own way of relating to clients, his own words and phrases, leaving little room for his students to study what Tommy had done and then adapt it to what would work long-term for them.

Two Big Problems With Farming

Hey, farming did work. Still does. You could become a successful real estate professional by following the path laid out by John Lumbleau, Tommy Hopkins and a few others. It was no longer just a matter of manipulative persuasion skills and sheer luck. It was now a matter of shoe leather and charm. You could become a champion. You could win love (and listings and sales) from the people in your "farm."

But there were a few severe problems. First and foremost…

Service-Oriented Marketing Principle #10:
Though it's important never to stop marketing yourself effectively, it's also important to do so in a way that burns up the least amount of your time and shoe leather.

Your time should be invested primarily in working on the specific needs of your clients, staying on top of your marketplace, studying changes in real estate law and practice, and meeting with people who matter. Spending half of your time out chit-chatting in the neighborhood is not the most efficient use of that time, nor is it even possible to continue doing that once the business starts to roll in.

And that brings up the second big problem:

Service-Oriented Marketing Principle #11:
You need to design a marketing program that you can keep going even when you get very, very busy with clients.

If you have a marketing program that you have to set aside when the business gets good, you'll be in bad shape—perhaps even having to start your marketing all over again when your business inevitably slows again.

There are other problems, of course. Not everyone is adept at knocking on doors and starting up witty conversations, and many people are even less happy about having their day interrupted by an unexpected knock at the front door than they are about unwanted telephone solicitations. As for me, in July of 1976, when I first made my way around my designated farm area, it was the sweaty Big Bad Wolf huffing and puffing his way from door to door, scaring the poor little homemakers out of their wits, and accomplishing very little.

A great thing happened to me, though. The city in which my "farm" was located passed an ordinance that outlawed door-to-door solicitation. At first, I thought I was doomed. This door-to-door thing was what I'd been taught to do in my company's fast-start training program. Now, I had to get creative. I had to dream up, very quickly, other ways to do my prospecting in my farm.

It was one of the best things that ever happened to me.

More New Developments

Though there really haven't been any comprehensive new programs like "farming" for many years, a variety of new techniques have arisen and had their moments in the sun. Some—like the machine that automatically dialed random telephone numbers in your area and sought appointments with a tape-recorded sales pitch—deserved to be buried and forgotten long before they actually were.

A new version of this is just now developing, in which companies pull in "live ones" via the Internet and pass them immediately to real estate professionals while they're still hot. While an improvement over random dialing, these techniques for luring clients can simply never replace the relationships that develop over time between potential clients and the professionals who contact them regularly through effective marketing programs. It is very telling that those who subscribe to Internet-based lead programs report that, at best, 12% of the leads actually turn into active clients. (Many say it's more like 5%.) These, obviously, are not the kind of "warm" leads we recently referred to.

Marketing techniques have also improved a bit because a great deal has been learned about what does and what does not work...what people do and do not remember, what does and what does not create a lasting positive image for the person marketing himself or herself, and more.

But most marketing still relies exclusively on Direct Response techniques and rests weakly on the real estate professional's sense of what he or she needs—i.e., clients—and doesn't begin with a close look at what the potential client needs, how the potential client operates, how to address what is really happening out in the world.

Paying attention to potential client needs and wishes is not rocket science. **Realize that you are not a house. You are a human with much to offer people who want or need to buy or sell a home.**

Further, there is this crucial issue: Are you developing a career? If so, everything you do should support the development of that career.

Much to our amazement, though—that is, to the amazement of Rand, Jill and myself—there just aren't any books or courses to be found on anything but Direct Response/short-term marketing. We're still stuck with fishing poles in our hands and inadequate bait on our hooks, when we could be gathering together a marketing program that does it all: builds our reputation, creates a large group of loyal clients and warm potential clients, and brings in a steady stream of very good income.

That, in the final analysis, is why we're in this business, and why this book had to be written.

CHAPTER SIX

Expectations: The Power Of the Possible, Or What Should You Expect From Your Marketing?

Okay, suppose a real estate guy—we'll call him Ralph Realtor—has placed a classified ad in the newspaper for a home he listed for sale. "CREAM PUFF!" the ad shouts. "Absolutely won't last" (which means, of course, that it is liable to sell very quickly, not that the home is about to fall over dead). "Perfect charmer for first-time buyers." (Uh-oh: "Charmer" is one of those dangerous words, usually intimating that the home is so small its occupants have to step outside to sneeze.) "Etc."

Ralph's word choice demonstrates that real estate classified ads haven't come far since Joe Doakes sat with his coffee cup at his metal desk in the 1960s. Nonetheless, Brenda Buyer calls Ralph on the phone and says, "Could you tell me something about this 'Cream Puff' you're advertising in the paper?"

Stop right here and notice something so important and so obvious that it's been overlooked by 99% of those who claim to be experts about marketing:

Brenda did not call and ask to speak with Ralph. She didn't call to ask Ralph to show her some houses or give her valuable advice. In fact, she had no idea whatsoever that she would get Ralph on the phone, much less who Ralph is. Quite simply, she called about a house in an advertisement, not about Ralph.

And Ralph, we will all agree, is not a house.

So how can Ralph generate phone calls from people asking for Ralph, not for information about a house?

Now, this sort of call is precisely what Ralph and all others expect to receive when they place their classified ads. As I've said, they fill the ads with zingy expressions, leave out crucial information so anyone interested will have to call, and wait anxiously by the phone for the fish to nibble. And if someone calls, the work begins, because Ralph's job is to transform someone who is vaguely but skeptically interested in a house mentioned in a classified ad into someone who is very specifically committed to working with Ralph in the complex and emotionally-taxing process of finding and buying a house.

Notice several things about this. First, Brenda—who may indeed have reached the stage where she would love to be working with a real estate professional she can trust and communicate effectively with—is throwing darts in the dark here. Second (and this is the other side of the same coin), Ralph is trying to bring in and take on a client who is in no way presold on the way he does business; so he is, with his classified ad, also throwing darts in the dark. It's all rather like a sloppily arranged marriage. The couple here is thrown into a room by little more than circumstance and expected to do a great job of handling one of the biggest, most intensely emotional, and most important decisions Brenda will ever make.

And sometimes it works, but sometimes it turns into a mess, and rarely does it result in an ideal relationship between client and real estate professional. Still, it's a valid way for Ralph to seek clients to work with, as is an open house or a classified ad.

All of these are forms of Direct Response Marketing—which is just about the only form of marketing that seems to be relevant to most of those who write marketing books and teach marketing courses.

There is, however, potentially far more to marketing than those using Direct Response Marketing ever even imagined possible.

So we ask: What do you expect from your marketing?

Hopefully, you expect far more than just one potential client, one telephone call from a reluctant stranger, one undefined "lead." Perhaps you have already learned to expect a great deal more than these possibilities. For example...

▶ 1. Your marketing should actually create and nourish the beginning of a relationship with potential clients whom you yourself may never have actually met. It is, therefore, a surrogate for you in the world that people can experience and come to appreciate and trust.

▶ 2. Your marketing should make you the big fish in your small pond—your target market. Or, if you will, your own "blue ocean," as W. Chan Kim and Renée Mauborgne suggest in *Blue Ocean Strategy.* You should become nearly famous. People should know who you are, how you do business, how easily they can relate to you, how active you are in the local marketplace, how deep your knowledge of real estate and real estate finance reaches, and how committed you are to serving your clients well, helping them achieve their goals and dreams.

▶ 3. Your marketing should provide those in your target market with "free samples" of who you are and how you do business, primarily by disseminating information that is potentially very relevant and valuable to them, even before they become your clients.

▶ 4. Your marketing should "position" you in the marketplace, making people very aware that you are the person to call if they need help in your areas of specialization, whether it's tax-deferred exchanges, selling homes in a specific development, finding the most affordable beach- or river-front properties, dealing with first-time buyers or helping immigrating Asians find a home for their extended families.

▶ 5. Your marketing should attract clients with whom you're most likely to get along well, people of like mind, people whose needs you can understand well, people who are inclined from the get-go to trust you and appreciate all that you have to offer.

▶ 6. Your marketing should create an automatic link in people's minds. If they think about anything relating to real estate, they should think about you and know how to contact you.

Remember:

Service-Oriented Marketing Principle #12:
You are not a house (though you may be,
I suppose, a comfy charmer).

You are yourself, a uniquely effective provider of service. Getting people to call on an advertisement or other marketing piece about YOU is a far different thing than getting people to call and ask a question about a "Cheap Charmer Nestled in Foothills." And since it is a far different thing…

- **You must approach this kind of marketing with very different expectations,**

- **You must measure the success of your marketing program differently, and**
- **You must work within different guidelines.**

About that second point.... When you submit a classified ad, it's potentially a one-shot deal. You can easily tell how well the ad works because you can count the number of telephone calls it generates. Compare that to the number of sales on the wall chart, and you can tell how well the agents in the office dealt with the phone calls (though we begin to get a little fuzzy with our quantification here). You can even compare what it cost to run the ad with how much income the ad generated and start talking about fancy things like return-on-investment in your marketing program.

But you can't do any of that stuff with much accuracy if you're purposefully marketing to build your own career, not just to get calls on a classified ad. You are marketing YOURSELF, not a house. The difference is huge. (And, as we'll shortly see, it gets even a bit more complex than this.)

Notice one other killer difference between these two modes of marketing. Someone who calls on a classified advertisement is looking in that section of the newspaper because he or she is at least mildly intrigued by the possibility of buying a house, yes? That's one of the main reasons that classified ads work rather well, though the road from initial phone call to trusting client relationship is very often a difficult one.

But when you send out marketing materials to your target market, the vast majority of those who receive what you send have no current need for nor interest in anyone's assistance with real estate matters. They're going to need your help—not now, but later—and it's likely that they don't know exactly when, any more than you do.

Why even bother with them, then? Because they will need your help sooner or later. And in the meantime, because you are constantly providing them with samples of the service you provide, they will build a relationship with you and they'll send friends, associates and family to you because you're the real estate professional they've come to trust.

The Roller Coaster vs. The Career

If you rely on Direct Response Marketing alone to bring in a continuing stream of business, you will almost certainly end up on a roller coaster, never confident that another transaction will follow the one you're just now completing. Again, Direct Response Marketing techniques are designed to bring in one call about one house. Where will the next call come from? A different classified ad? The next open house you hold? An office walk-in? Maybe.

Notice, though, that there is an inherent elegance and simplicity to marketing to motivate people to want to work specifically with you, rather than marketing a home and trying to sneak yourself in as the person's real estate agent in the process. There is also a geometric expansion, similarly elegant, in which one client who has come to you because of the effectiveness of your marketing tends to refer many more clients to you.

In the first case, using Direct Response Marketing and nothing else, you have turned your career, as I've suggested earlier, into a kind of simplistic fishing trip. You go to the same fishing hole, use the same lures, and wait, hoping for a nibble that you, if you are lucky and skillful, can bring to the surface. It's a waiting game involving a lot of luck, and with very little responsiveness to changing market conditions.

In the second case, still using Direct Response Marketing, but also using Service-Oriented Marketing, your eyes remain on the goal. You're building and nourishing a career with your every working day and with your every marketing program and marketing piece. It all comes together for you over time, and business gets better and better—so long as your marketing program remains one of the most important things you do, something you are dedicated to, something you truly own in every way.

I will tell you briefly of a process that brought me my own first experience of wealth.

I began as a real estate agent in Southern Orange County in 1976. I worked with one of the major brokerages because it offered a two-week training program. I knew next to nothing about real estate law or finance, about selling houses, about attracting and working with clients. And I knew virtually no one in the city where I started out as a real estate agent. In short, I have no idea why the company hired me—except for their recognition that I believed I could do this thing and do it profitably and well. That, in fact, was my expectation.

I was, in any case, totally reliant on marketing to bring in clients. So I went at it with a great deal of energy. I took on a development called Village San Juan, about 600+ homes of various styles in a low- to mid-priced (relatively speaking) development in San Juan Capistrano. My manager called it a "bread-and-butter farm," meaning the low prices on the homes would theoretically require me to work twice as hard to make the same amount of commission money as those in the office who worked higher-priced homes—but it was expected that the homes in my area would turn over more frequently than would luxury homes.

Whatever the case, I was reasonably happy with my target market. I started distributing a monthly newsletter and also a monthly sheet that told what homes were selling for in the area that month and also relayed matters of specific relevance to the neighborhood where I was working. I also started doing a few "break-into-my-target-market's-consciousness" events and programs. In 1976, our nation guided its lunar landing module on to the moon, a large step for mankind (as you may recall, if you're old enough), so I bought over 600 tiny moon cacti in little plastic containers, planted a cocktail toothpick next to each cactus with an American flag on it, and gave one to each household in Village San Juan. (The regional manager for the real estate company, by the way, asked my office manager to let him know how many listings and sales my cacti brought in. Answer: For six months, none. Thereafter, nearly every time people asked me to come by and list their home for sale, they pointed to the now-slightly-larger moon cactus in their kitchen window and said, "Oh, by the way. Thanks.") It takes a while for a cactus to grow.

On every piece of paper I gave to the residents of my target market, I referred to myself as The Village San Juan Specialist. I backed that up with every piece of information about the area I could find.

I continued doing this kind of thing for months. I really had no idea of how successful my marketing was until I had been doing it for very nearly six months. I could have stopped many times before then, utterly frustrated and convinced that the whole thing was a total loss. I was fortunate in that I had mentors—other real estate professionals in the office who were watching my work appreciatively, cheering me on, assuring me that I'd start reaping the rewards from all of this work by the end of my sixth month. (Why six months? I'm still not sure, nor do I think it's a necessary rule. But we'll talk about it further in coming pages.)

My accountant, looking at the obvious lack of income over the course of my first months in real estate, was kind enough to suggest that I explore other modes of employment. "Ever consider pumping gas, Bill? You might be good at it."

I turned to a couple of the real estate professionals I most admired, despairing of ever seeing any results. "It just isn't working for me," I whined. "I guess I just wasn't cut out to do this."

What did they do? They laughed at me. "You're doing everything right," they declared. "You'd be a complete fool to stop now."

They were right.

I'm sure I've been a complete fool many times in my life, but thankfully, not this time. I hung in there. After a short time, people from my target market were calling, talking to me as if I were an old friend, asking me for help in deciding whether to sell their home, whether to buy an investment property nearby, whether I might help their brother from Akron, Ohio, find a good home in San Juan Capistrano. I had people quoting my newsletter back to me, forgetting that I was the writer of the valued information. I had people pointing me out to friends in restaurants: "Pssst! He's the Village San Juan Specialist."

I had a great time. I made more money than I ever imagined I could. And I had the pleasure of making a genuine contribution to a lot of lives.

Experience made me a believer: Raise your expectations to the sky! And keep on keeping on.

PART TWO

The Conceptual Ingredients Of Service-Oriented Marketing

CHAPTER SEVEN
Time And Repetition

L et's pause for a moment for another true tale.

An agent in my office many years ago decided to try this sort of marketing. She created a contest that invited children to submit an essay about their parents, stating why their parents deserved a night out together. The winning entry was to receive a dinner for two and, if I remember correctly, the fee for a babysitter. Good idea.

We'll call this agent Shelly. She went to the trouble to make up a very attractive flyer, sent it out to about three hundred households that she decided made up her target market, and waited for the entries to pour in.

When the final day of the contest rolled around, Shelly had received only two entries (which is actually a reasonably good response, as any marketing expert will tell you). She bristled at the idea of going ahead and paying for someone's night out when there were only two contestants, but she did so. "But that proves it," she declared. "This kind of marketing doesn't work for me."

And in truth, her experience did prove something—but not that this kind of marketing didn't work for her. It proved that this kind of marketing requires a substantial amount of time and repetition.

Service-Oriented Marketing Principle #13:
Time, consistency and repetition are absolutely essential for a successful service-oriented marketing program.

Notice something: Even though she had never sent anything to her target market before, Shelly could have made this contest work if she had sent out at least four different flyers about the contest, one each month, and one more reminder a week before the contest ended. Further, she could have created a link with a fine local restaurant— where the winners would be sent—and had the restaurant feature a small display that promoted the contest, and she could have included stories about the restaurant and its staff in her promotional flyers for the contest.

My point at its simplest is this:

Service-Oriented Marketing Principle #14:
Direct response marketing is a vehicle with limited returns and a narrow range of activities... a part of, but never all of, our personal marketing program.

You need more.

Marketing to build and nourish your career is a very different matter. You need to know who you are, you need to know what you're doing, you need to do your marketing well and often and consistently, and over time, you will come to own your target market.

And here, the adventure gets exciting!

CHAPTER EIGHT

Why Should Someone Call Upon A Real Estate Professional?

Let's start with a couple of widely-held incorrect answers to that question.

First, people used to call on real estate professionals because that was the only way to access the area's multiple listing service. If you were selling your home, you wanted to put the entire local real estate community to work on bringing buyers to look at the property. The way to do that was to get listed in the MLS. If you were buying a home, you wanted to see all the homes that were currently on the market, so you needed access to a real estate agent who had a copy of the latest MLS book with all the area's active listings.

In many cases, a real estate professional earned his or her commission essentially by belonging to the multiple listing service and helping to put it to work for you as you bought or sold a home. Today, however, buyers or sellers of real estate can often access the multiple listing service and other displays of listings on the Internet and, increasingly, that is precisely what they do. It is therefore no longer possible to make money simply by belonging to the MLS. And that, as we will see, is a good thing for both real estate professionals and their clients and potential clients.

Second, it was once assumed that people needed a forcefully manipulative salesperson in order to get the best price for their home or to negotiate the lowest purchase price for the buyer. This has changed. A real estate professional should not be a silly doormat, of course; he or she should be an advocate for his or her client's needs and interests. But real estate has become far more sophisticated than it used to be. Though people will benefit by buying and selling with the guidance of a professional, they are certainly not incapable of gathering the needed data and finding out what a particular house should sell for in the day's market. No amount of arm-twisting can obscure or overwhelm real market data. What the public needs, therefore, is informed, knowledgeable guidance in a process that most buyers and sellers know far more about than they used to.

Market research published by the National Association of Realtors® and personal experience of real estate transactions shows that the public turns to a real estate professional for assistance when buying or selling real estate for the following reasons:

▶ **1. They Want Service:** A real estate professional who can be trusted and related to well can provide the kind of service in a huge and complex transaction that will maximize profits, save unneeded expenses, avoid potential pitfalls, and make a potentially unpleasant and frightening experience as user-friendly as possible.

▶ **2. They Want Guidance:** A knowledgeable real estate professional who listens carefully to their needs and wishes can be an enormous asset in making the right choices and staying away from legal and financial hassles.

▶ **3. They Want Help In Translating Their Needs And Wishes Into Reality:** It simply isn't easy to turn an abstract picture of the home a person wants into actual sticks and bricks. It isn't easy to enter a particular neighborhood and discover its strengths and weaknesses as rapidly as possible. It isn't easy to make a rational decision about an inherently emotional matter. A trusted real estate professional can help immensely.

▶ **4. They Want Advocacy:** If something goes wrong in a transaction, buyers and sellers need an advocate who will stand up for them in everything from incipient legal disputes (though not, emphatically, as their attorney, but as a crucial member of their support team) to debates over who should get the chandelier in the hallway.

▶ **5. They Want To Be Genuinely Heard:** A real estate professional who is sympathetic to and compassionate with his or her clients will add an extraordinary human dimension to a potentially difficult experience, will speed everything up because he or she is well aware of what the clients truly want, and will help sidestep problems that can be avoided because of having the clients' needs accurately in mind.

There are, indeed, a vast number of important qualities that a real estate professional can and generally does bring to a transaction:

Accuracy, speed, better profit, better purchase price, more solid transaction. But the key element is service.

Service-Oriented Marketing Principle #15:
It is because of superior service that the best real estate careers thrive.

Here's a crucial question: **How Do People Choose Their Real Estate Professional?**

In professional surveys, we've seen that more people base their choice on reputation than on anything else. Are you known for the good service you provide? Is your name synonymous with good real estate practice? More to the point, perhaps: What can you do to develop and enrich a good and unique reputation?

We had a client who was using one of our prospecting newsletters with great impatience. "I don't care about the information in the newsletter all that much," she said. "I want to be sure that, even if the newsletter only gets glanced at on its way to the kitchen trash can, they see my face and my name." So every month she called and demanded that we make her picture larger on the front of her newsletter, and she'd raise the size of the type for her name and for her slogan ("The name of success!").

Now, I may be wrong about this—but I doubt it, because I heard it from people who received her newsletter. The larger her photo became, the more it seemed to overwhelm those who looked at the newsletter even for a moment. It wasn't a good marketing move. It seemed to threaten to reach off the page and grab people by the throat. And the slogan was about the real estate professional, not about the quality of the experience clients could expect. (This, by the way, is a simple definition of the marketing term, "promise.")

My point here is that people choose their real estate professional because, by reputation, that person is going to make their transaction go the right way. They will bring sellers the best price for their home. They will help negotiate the best possible selling price and terms for their buyers. And they will be very pleasant to work with, trustworthy in every respect.

The actual bottom line, though, is:

Service-Oriented Marketing Principle #16a:
We develop our reputation through our marketing …through the pieces of ourselves, the embodiments of the kind of service we provide, that we send out into our target market..

Though I have never seen this at the core of a book or course on marketing, the conclusion thus far should be fairly obvious:

Service-Oriented Marketing Principle #16b:
If people want service above all from their real estate professional, your marketing program should provide service, above all.

Your reputation will grow as your business grows and your business grows as your reputation grows.

CHAPTER NINE

Why Should Someone Choose You?

This is another absolutely crucial point that I have never seen appropriately discussed in a book or course on marketing, though the words come down to us from antiquity:

Remember Service-Oriented Marketing Principle #2?

Know thyself!

Without a good awareness of who you are, what you like, how you like to work, and what matters to you, you are extremely ill-prepared to answer this crucial question: Why should someone want to call upon YOU to assist him or her with a real estate transaction?

Again, there have been some pretty flimsy but widely-held answers to that question. Perhaps the most common, even semi-conscious answer is: "Because I'm a good person and I need money (that is, commission checks)."

Obviously, that isn't quite substantial enough a reason for someone thinking of selling a million dollar home to list it with you, quite possibly paying a $30,000 commission to you and your brokerage upon the close of the deal.

So let's ask again. What is it specifically about YOU that is worth about $30,000 in the successful purchase or sale of a million dollar home?

Phrased this way, the question brings up a large range of related questions. For example, it is reasonably likely that we'll see further changes to the way real estate professionals are compensated. What, really, do we do with the question, "Is the real estate professional's work in the sale of a million dollar home worth five times more than the work involved in the sale of a two hundred thousand dollar home?"

As this book is being written, a revolution in real estate practices is gaining speed. Compensation practices are already changing. The effects of computerizing all aspects of a deal and coordinating everything from loan to title search to property inspections are about to explode into a much faster and more efficient way of selling homes. Ties with other communities, other states and even other countries are exploding the real estate market into a global network of opportunity.

It is all extraordinarily exciting, but none of it changes any of the principles in this book at all.

So let me say it again. You need to know yourself. You need to take a personal inventory, including your religious beliefs, personal philosophy, social groups, activities for fun and entertainment, and on and on. What makes you tick? What do you do whenever you have the chance? What are you passionate about? What do you love?

It would be very helpful, too, to indulge in one or more of the gauges of character and personality (like, for example, the Myers-Briggs personality assessment analysis) to find out how you tend to problem solve, to seek rewards, to relate to people, etc.

Brief digression: I am a right-brained type for whom exact figures are aggravations to be rounded up. A room is about nine feet by twelve feet—that's an adequate description for me. I may show up later with a piece of paper that I've scribbled my desk dimensions on and a tape measure to make sure the desk will fit into the room. Or I may not.

Fairly early in my experience as a real estate professional, I found myself showing property to an engineer who always brought along his tape measure, his calculator, even an old slide rule (on his belt, no less), and a notebook. This was rather alien behavior to me; it made little sense.

If he asked the dimensions of a room and I told him, "About nine by twelve," he'd frown at me and shake his head, pull out his tape measure and rapidly measure the room down to the nearest eighth of an inch.

Thankfully, I was taking a course in personality types at the time. So I reacted to what seemed to me an infuriating, anally-retentive tendency to want everything in its most detailed measurements with more patience than I otherwise would have. This man, whom I truly grew to like immensely, simply needed life to work that way. And my job was to meet his needs. So when he wanted to know the rating of the insulation in each of the walls, the floor and ceiling, I got the information for him.

Perhaps even more to the point, I became more aware of my own personality type and my own needs, and thus more forgiving of what might have seemed like my own sloppy thinking at times, among the other quaint and unproductive traits I possess.

But I digress.

Service-Oriented Marketing Principle #17:
Your marketing program is built on
who you are.

One of the first things you will need to do as you construct (or reconstruct) your marketing program is to figure out who should be part of your target market and who should not. Start with this awareness: People who share some or all of the passionate interests and beliefs that you have are the most likely by a long shot to call on you for assistance with their real estate transactions and to have a rich, positive experience of you.

Let's be clear about this. Outside of the different approach to precision and order, my engineer client and I were extremely compatible. We enjoyed not only the process of discovering the best way to sell his home together and to find and buy the next one, but also the process of getting to know one another. So we're not talking about making sure you only work with people who are exactly like you. It's a deeper matter than that.

We're talking about working with people who are genuinely compatible, open to who you are, appreciative of how you work, your integrity, your sense of humor, your abilities and knowledge.

Obviously, it makes the most sense to market to those who are the most likely to respond—and even more sense to market to those who are most likely to respond positively…people who feel immediately inclined to like and trust you. My engineer client responded immediately to my sense of integrity and lack of selfishness.

Now, it may be that the main thing you have in common with your target market is that you live in the same development that most of the people in your target market do. Perhaps you have a "farm." The very successful real estate professional and trainer Danielle Kennedy constantly stressed her slogan, "I live where I work."

But the ideal, if possible, is to find a way to market to like-minded people who live in your area. (You can, of course, find a way to combine a growing list of like-minded people with a list of people who live in one specific neighborhood or development, if you choose.) If you are extremely active in your church, for example, this can be your basic target market.

Ah—do I sense a little resistance to that idea? Something about keeping business and personal beliefs separate? Something about never imposing upon people in your social or spiritual group? If so, it's time for an extremely important pep talk.

One of the most unpleasant experiences of my life was the dinner at the home of a friend who, once the dishes were cleared, brought out his seminar materials—his charts and graphs—and began a pitch about a multilevel marketing (or "network marketing") program. I felt like sludge. I felt I was invited to this dinner for no reason other than a sales pitch. The evening turned dark, indeed.

But this is as far from what I'm talking about as Pluto is from the sun. Please understand this vastly important point.

Service-Oriented Marketing Principle #18:
Service-oriented marketing doesn't irritate, it provides valued service.

Thus, what you do and provide are welcomed by almost all of those who receive the service. You are not trying to get people to do something they are reluctant to do. You are providing service.

For example, if you choose your church as your target market, you may be motivated to create a church festival that brings a good amount of money and people into the church and gives the church very positive exposure. You may want to involve yourself in some of the church's important activities. You may wish to be on the church's board of directors. (Think this over carefully, though. Members of the board are often right at the center of all an organization's controversies, and you can end up making unnecessary enemies.) In all cases, you are serving the church and its congregation and, arguably, its mission.

You may ask people you know in the church if you can send them a monthly newsletter that you believe they'll enjoy and possibly even benefit from. In time, you will very likely be mailing your monthly newsletter to nearly all of the congregation—and you will be assisting many of them in their real estate transactions.

But that is only one example. Perhaps you love to play tennis, or perhaps golf. The associated clubs make great target markets. Perhaps you are involved in local government; a target market can be created from those who are involved in local government with you.

A friend, once the head of a crisis center that fields phone calls from people in emotional distress, decided that her target market was sophisticated environmentalists. Her slogan is "Sustainable Real Estate for a Sustainable Community." To many in the real estate profession, this sounds like about as good an idea as telephone pole sitting. Most people believe that your marketing should cast the widest possible net, not limit itself to a group of people who aren't exactly the meat and potatoes of the real estate profession. This is often totally incorrect.

My friend markets to a large and very specific community, it turns out. She sends out materials that would be considered much too far to the left for many homeowners. But she has a big, enthusiastic following—and does an extremely solid business. She also does such unusual things as taking a full month off every year, sometimes to do volunteer work abroad. She walks her talk...and lives her life with passion.

Her success flies in the face of the belief that you must make every effort to offend no one because you may lose potential clients. The fact is, you should be yourself in this business—give people the genuine article—because that is how you will attract the people who will most value what you have to give as a real estate professional... the people who will remain your clients for life and will send you referrals constantly. Also, you should be aware that you really aren't saying anything that will attract the attention of the "right" people if you aren't occasionally risking offending the "wrong" people.

If you send out bland, faceless marketing materials, no one will notice them anyway. No one will respond.

In an article on the extraordinarily successful marketing techniques employed by the beauty and health products company, Aveda, Danielle Sacks (writing in *FastCompany*) placed this first on the list: "Stand up for your beliefs. Afraid to alienate any customer, most brands stay bland. Aveda's strong stance on beauty extends through its products' pores to its customers." And live those beliefs, Sacks adds. "Aveda not only makes sure its business practices are eco-friendly, but its everyday practices as well."

Of course, this doesn't mean you should rub people's noses in your beliefs. If Linus (of the *Peanuts* comic strip) were a real estate professional, he would be ill-advised to lead people into the pumpkin patch every year in anticipation of seeing the return of the Great Pumpkin. The point isn't to create weird controversy with questionable activities, even if those activities attract one or two devotees. The point, really, is to be who you are, and to do so publicly, so that people with similar values and mindsets will know to call on you if they want help with a real estate matter.

The mere fact that you are ready and willing to stand up as exactly who you are will make you unique, set you apart and cause people to take interest in you.

So…in answer to the question: Why should people call specifically on YOU for assistance with their real estate transactions?

▶ 1. Because they have been experiencing you as a provider of service through your marketing materials and through the services that you provide them.

▶ 2. Because they know from the materials you've been sending them that you are knowledgeable and good at what you do, and that they can very likely relate to you well.

▶ 3. Because they know from your reputation and their experience of you in your marketing that you are someone they will probably feel good about working with—a like-minded person who listens deeply and compassionately.

Mixing Business and Personal

We have long assumed, most of us, that it is dangerous to mix business and personal life. We don't tell our clients and customers about our gall bladder operations, generally speaking. They don't need to know about our tendency to get depressed in the months of winter, either, or that we're haunted by memories of an abusive uncle.

But wait. Don't assume people will be offended by news of what is happening in your life, even if it is traumatic. Remember: People are drawn to work with professionals they can relate to. They want to do business with someone who is likely to understand their needs and wishes.

I had an experience in spring of 1992 that completely revised my sense of mixing my personal life with my business life. My wife Beverly died in open heart surgery and my writing schedule was such that I had to produce an issue of a newsletter—*The Wednesday Wrap*, which went out to thousands of readers, distributed by various title insurance companies—a few days after her death. I had, in the past, revealed some of my personal experiences in the pages of this letter, especially those that might make my readers laugh. As one long-term reader said to me not long ago, "You made all of us readers feel like members of your extended family."

This is a matter of style and taste. Some professionals wish to remain very private. Others of us want to know what lights up the dashboards of our clients and are, in turn, very ready to divulge details of who we are. So here I was faced with what seemed an overwhelming question at the time: Do I say anything about my wife's death in this newsletter?

I did. The reaction was immediate. I received cards, phone messages, books on grieving, and, most amazingly, the inquiries about my prospecting newsletters increased beyond belief. I took a little time away, leaving the office telephone in the hands of the person who became my assistant in the business (and then my partner, and after six years, my wife, Robyn), and I recall her phoning me in Boulder, where I was visiting my brother.

"How many requests for samples of the newsletters do you normally get?" she asked.

"Maybe three a week," I said.

"How about thirty a day?" she responded.

Three things immediately became clear. First, my sense that human beings, given half a chance, are essentially kind and supportive is correct. People respond to genuinely-expressed truths of the heart. Second, occasional bits of personal information are actually a good thing in one's marketing program. And third, this isn't something you want to do at such an intense level very often—only when it's true and you can hardly avoid it.

Here, in any case, is what I wrote in my newsletter to my "extended family":

My wife did not survive her operation (on 4/9). She was to have three heart valve transplants…her third open heart surgery. At the point in the operation when they tried to get her off the bypass machine and back on her own heart/lung power, her body went into a toxic reaction, her blood lost the ability to clot…and so it went—so she went. Though—miraculously—she is still so very much with me, and with so many.

Here is the amazing thing. I have lived for 12 wondrous years with this gentle, extraordinarily loving woman, and during that time, the thing I most feared—my biggest fear in the whole world—was that I would "lose" her. Her history of heart problems meant that we could never forget her mortality. It also meant that we could never forget how fortunate we were to spend another day together. We wasted very little time, and were together as much as we could possibly be. It has been 12 years of astonishing growth, as if we had worked (and played) together from emotional preschool to a few stringent graduate courses…and passed all the tests.

The amazing thing, in any case, is that the eventuality I most feared has not left me utterly incapacitated, empty, wanting only to die, as I had anticipated it would. To the absolute contrary, it has left me feeling very full—of gratitude, primarily—feeling very capable, wanting to live my life to the fullest. To continue learning, to take in all the beauty there is to see, and to see it with eyes that somehow serve not only myself but also the person who taught me so much about beauty.

I feel, oddly, like a valuable person at this moment. My perspective on things is radically different from the day-to-day perspective most of us walk around with. I am, admittedly, just emerging from a pained state of shock—but I also feel: (1) No patience for trivia and time- and mind-wasting (how can I say this delicately?) bullslop. (For example, I'm finding it next to impossible to follow—to care about—the current political campaigns…or any of what the local tv stations call the "news," for that matter.) (2) A tremendous desire to reach out honestly to people, to cut through all the social niceties, the pleasantries, the fibs and the balderdash. (3) An overwhelming need to simply watch a cloud, listen to a beautiful symphony, read a wonderful book, paint and write, and engage in long conversations with dear friends, the kinds of conversations that are full to the brim of mental and emotional "Ah-ha's" and laughter and deeply-felt connections.

• *I've been noticing that the greatest percentage of people on this planet are extremely compassionate and kind—that so many people have treated me with sincere care. (I recall seeing a car teetering over a bridge on a freeway, and people rushing to help without even thinking about it.) What gets in the way, usually, is fear…and when someone is going through as profound and traumatic an experience as I have been, people seem to cut right through their usual fears and self-consciousness and act lovingly.*

• *From my current perspective, most of the fears that cause us to believe "it's a dog-eat-dog-world" and make us treat one another as potential enemies are illusions. (I mean, what can you say to a man who has lost what he most feared losing? That he'd better be real careful or he'll lose something important?)*

• *Also from my current perspective, there is nothing real that you can lose. This is a tough one to explain—and not really appropriate material for a real estate newsletter. Or perhaps, as I think about it, there could be few subjects more appropriate for a real estate and economic newsletter. Perhaps, in fact, our sense of "economics" and "security" could benefit from a little reflection.*

I spent a good deal of time with my grandfather, a very successful CPA, in the years before he died. I noticed that he was proud of his career—but what he really wanted to talk about were the vacations he took with his family, the times at Catalina, the trips to Europe he and his wife took with me, the names of the hotels we stayed in and the foods we loved the most, the seas we swam in and the crazy way I dragged him through the Prado and every other art museum wherever we went. I've watched my father—who made himself a millionaire and was a masterful business executive—lose all of the possessions he acquired, sitting confused in an empty room, ravaged by Alzheimer's Disease…and my mother, wondering at a life that didn't turn out the way she thought it would. If I could give each of you just one thing at this moment, this is what it would be: Be clear on what matters to you most in your life, and don't make it secondary to the earning of money and paying of mortgages and trimming of taxes and protecting yourself from business competitors—all the stuff that really is secondary. Love what you love, feel what you feel, know what you know, and live every moment consciously. There is really nothing else to do!

CHAPTER TEN
Expanding The Scope Of Your Service

You undoubtedly know that a married couple who file their taxes jointly and who have owned and lived in a personal residence for two years or more during the past five years and haven't used this exclusion for at least 24 months can exclude up to $500,000 in gains from the sale of that personal residence from taxation. This is one of the most wonderful ways in which real estate offers particularly attractive tax benefits.

No doubt your clients know this as well—at least, in general terms. But do they really? A friend recently told me about a special tax rule that allows people over 62 to avoid paying taxes on a certain amount of the profit from their home sale if they've owned the house for at least a year. It was nonsense, of course, but it was a reasonable facsimile of what she'd been told. Just to send her a newsletter that straightens out the home sale gains exclusion, therefore, would be an immense service to this person.

People are similarly grateful to learn that the two years in which they occupy the personal residence can be an aggregate, not necessarily a consecutive period of 24 months, from the past five years. Maybe, for example, they lived in the home four or five years ago, then sold it after it was rented out for nearly three years. They still qualify for the $500,000 exclusion.

Maybe they didn't even own it for the first year they lived in it, then they bought it and rented it out, then moved in for another year and a half. That, too, qualifies for the $500,000 exclusion.

Obviously, there are hundreds of strategies that can be engineered for saving taxes in the purchase and sale of real estate. There are ways of maximizing the selling price of a home (which include, as you doubtless know, setting the price right at market, an act that, as studies show, usually brings in the highest price when a transaction is negotiated).

There are also ways of making your home as safe and energy-efficient as possible. There are, in fact, endless numbers of things most potential homebuyers and current homeowners could benefit from knowing. How do you let people know that you are aware of all of this—that you are the one who can help guide them to the most efficient uses of their money, and the most beneficial purchase and sale transactions?

Service-Oriented Marketing Principle #19: Give the information away!

Consistently, every month (or, in the case of newspaper columns, every week), you give out "free samples" of the kind of information and guidance you are ready to provide.

That is the heart of the service-oriented marketing program you develop and stay with. It is also, as we'll explore in a moment, a constant example of "Show—Don't Tell," three of the most important words to anyone engaged in marketing himself or herself.

Most people are very willing to give away freebies if they lead to a sale. But I want you to take that idea a step further. Ideally, giving out helpful information becomes a knee-jerk reaction for successful real estate professionals.

There are people who write monthly investment newsletters, sometimes charging hundreds, even thousands, of dollars for a year's subscription. How do they gain clients? Increasingly, they do so by giving away bits of information whenever they can. They offer, for example, daily analyses of the investment markets, emailed for free to people who aren't even paying for subscriptions to any of their products. The daily commentary is rather entertaining, full of "attitude," and it gives you a definite idea over time of the philosophy of the writer. It also gives away a lot of helpful tips. For example, the email might suggest that gold is about to gain in value and discuss why. The writer may hold back the names of his or her favorite gold investments—the coins, mining stocks, and mutual funds that might gain the most from gold's rise. For that, you subscribe to the writer's newsletter.

Happily, as a real estate professional, there isn't much you have to "hold back." You make your living by guiding people through successful transactions, so you can give away the Informational Farm, so to speak, without giving away what people will gladly pay you for.

Notice: You are giving away helpful information. This is one of the key things you do as a professional—provide the needed information, make suggestions, point people in the right direction, give out ideas that your clients can take to their tax and legal advisors to put into action. So you are giving away service.

Service is what you're all about. People will notice. They'll want more. They'll call on you for any assistance they might need in the world of real estate.

CHAPTER ELEVEN
Show, Don't Tell

Y ou cannot tell anyone how wonderful you are. It just doesn't work.

But real estate professionals attempt to do just that in their advertising all the time. Their ads will very likely stress how many million dollars' worth of homes they have sold in the past year, how many homes they listed, how many exclusive Platinum Potato plaques their company has awarded them, and on and on.

These are not entirely irrelevant pieces of information, but they miss the mark if they are all you're telling the world. So you had a zillion deals last year. Did your clients benefit from your service, energy and expertise? Were they happy? Would they recommend you to others?

Take a deep breath and realize the truth: You can't answer those questions credibly yourself. You can't say, "My clients are 74% happier than those of other agents." Above all, you can't say: "I'm the professional you should call." That is, you can't say it with any credibility.

Service-Oriented Marketing Principle #20:
You can show; you can't tell. You can, though, tell your story…and your clients can, in testimonials, say things credibly that you can't say about yourself.

You can show people that you are the professional they should call. Show, don't tell. You see? Mrs. Fennwackle, your tenth grade English teacher, was right—especially when it comes to marketing. Show the people, don't tell them.

Provide service in your marketing materials. Send out pieces of your knowledge, your experience, your character and personality.

You can provide seminars on important topics, hold classes for first-time buyers on how to purchase a home, coach people on what to do if their expenses are spinning out of control and it looks like they might lose their home, team up with a tax advisor and give a workshop on strategies for reducing tax liability in the sale of highly-appreciated properties. You can provide introductory workshops on building wealth through real estate and relevant financing, perhaps working as a real estate professional and mortgage professional duo—giving the workshops to people in your target market and perhaps elsewhere.

You can run a weekly column in a local newspaper with news, tips, hints regarding saving and making money, avoiding legal or tax hassles, and other real estate-related matters. You can send newsletters—ideally, once each and every month—to the people in your target market, filled with information and occasional reasons to chuckle. You can send out notes to people on their birthdays or other important occasions.

In all cases, you are showing you are knowledgeable and committed to providing the best service by doing precisely that—for free, for your clients and potential clients, constantly and consistently throughout the year.

And, as Principle #20 states, there's something else you can do. You can let others talk about how wonderful you are.

There is tremendous credibility in testimonials. Truly, there are few forms of marketing that are more powerful than the words of happy, satisfied, enthusiastic clients. You can print those words (maybe even with a photo of the clients and their new home) in your newsletter. You can create flyers filled with testimonials. You can create print ads—for local newspapers or magazines—that are built around testimonials. And you can fill your website with testimonials.

I am particularly keen on the way my colleague, Jill, gains and uses testimonials for our business. We work very hard at practicing what we preach. Since we often advocate the use of testimonials, it makes sense that we use them extensively ourselves. There is a good, juicy testimonial on the back page of every monthly newsletter we ourselves send out to our many clients. You'll find a remarkably lengthy group of testimonials on our website, too (*www.rightsidemarketing.com*).

What I'm suggesting here is that you combine the power of testimonials with all the other marketing that you do. Sprinkle testimonials like delicious spice on all your marketing pieces. Testimonials don't quite stand up as the sole focus of marketing pieces (unless we're considering very small print ads, or ads that seek to lead people to your website—more on that one soon, in our discussion of the Internet—in which case they can work wonders).

You can't say, "I'm your best choice." Your actions can say it, however, and the words of happy clients can, too. Indeed, both can say it with utter credibility. If a stranger walks on to the tennis court, he will be believed if he says he has a whopper of a serve if he serves a few before opening his mouth. Indeed, if he's right, others will say it for him.

How Do You Obtain Testimonials?

When you make a follow-up call to clients after a recently-completed transaction, ask them for their comments on what you did well and what you could improve on. They are usually very ready to provide such information, so be sure you have a notepad when you ask the question. And take the best notes you can.

When they're through, jot down a few sentences that resemble some of the things they said and repeat those sentences back to the client, asking if they are a good representation of what the client said. Let the client edit the sentences a bit, then ask permission to use their name and their words in your personal marketing materials. Most people will very readily grant that permission.

You may also find excellent little testimonials in the thank-you notes from clients and other communications—even cursory emails. Copy those down, too, and then call the clients and ask if you can name them and use their words in your personal marketing materials.

This is crucial: **Always Be Sure You Get Permission To Use Their Words.** Never use a testimonial that you have no permission to use. It's more than a mere courtesy. It is the responsible and ethical way to treat your clients' words.

Those words can prove very valuable to you.

The Power Of Story

I should also add that relating who you are as a professional through stories is almost always far more powerful than just trying to say how wonderful you are. Further, stories can provide an education regarding various aspects of real estate transactions.

As we will see later, a relatively new form of marketing is growing up on the Internet. Real estate professionals are "blogging"—creating on-going journals filled with a wide variety of information and, most often, a series of stories relating recent experiences in the business. This conveys valuable information, builds a relationship between the reader and the real estate professional, and gives the reader a sense of the real estate professional's qualities. It's another form of "show— don't tell."

CHAPTER TWELVE

Consistency

Though it is important for your potential clients to see your name and face in many contexts, one of the crucial elements of a successful marketing program is consistency. You should, for example, have a main photo that you use on everything. You can occasionally use other photos within your newsletters, for example, but you want the same photo on the front page every month, month after month. And you want the photo to look like you, not like a prom queen or king twenty years younger than you.

So—you've gone through the arduous task of answering the questions, "Who am I?" "What makes me tick?" "What brings me true and lasting pleasure?" "What do I believe in?" Now you're ready to build a marketing program that is, in every respect, in harmony with all you found in your self-assessment.

Design it. Build it. Decide who will receive materials from you regularly, and what those materials will be, and how you're going to get them out—without fail...and without unnecessary expenditures of time, energy or money.

Then—start it.

Then—stay with it. And be consistent. Don't send your newsletters out on brown paper one month, gray the next. Allow people to start knowing it's your newsletter the moment they see it in the mail. Even more important: Don't change your marketing program unless you're sure something isn't working. Be patient, confident, consistent.

Consistent in appearance, consistent in timing, consistent in tone, consistent in content, consistent in sophistication. It is tempting to change things periodically—and may seem a good way to keep refreshing the program and holding on to your clients' and potential clients' interest. But the proven fact is, just as CocaCola stays with its well-known logo (and gets into big trouble if it drops its classic formula), you and your materials will be best recognized and most memorable if you resist the temptation to change. Remain consistent.

My accountant has built her career on the quality of her work and on her hats. Really! She says her husband suggested this, way back when they had no money and they were trying to build her business. "You love hats! Why don't you wear a hat?" he said. "Why don't you get your head examined?" most people would have responded...but Patricia caught the message quickly.

She became the only accountant in town who always wore a stylish hat. Always. It became her trademark. When she eventually placed a weekly column in the local newspaper, her photo showed the Lady-in-the-Hat. When you saw her at a community event, she was immediately recognizable as the Lady-in-the-Hat.

She had the added benefit of being named Patricia Bliss and having a personality that rivaled sunshine after a rainstorm. But she was known—and indeed, she was and is known throughout her target market—for her hats.

Last holiday season, her office sent out a card with a photo of the entire staff, which has grown to a remarkable size, and all the women who work with Patricia were wearing hats. This is someone who knows how to market.

Creating a trademark or logo or slogan or all of the above is a great idea—if it is positive and catches people's imaginations and truly represents your personality and character—but it won't work unless you use it consistently, making as few changes as possible. And make sure you give your marketing time to work its way into the awareness and imaginations of those in your target market.

CHAPTER THIRTEEN
Amp-It-Up

Still…you may wonder, justifiably, if there aren't things you can do to hasten the success of your marketing program a bit. Indeed, there are! Let's look at a bunch of proven ways of amping up your program without changing it.

First, find ways to meet or meet with potential clients.

You can hold workshops, as mentioned earlier. You can call people whose names appear in newspapers, who deserve a word of thanks or congratulations, who are doing a service to the community. You can also get involved in local service organizations.

Second, call for feedback or participation.

Remember Shelly's dinner-for-two contest? You can build a promotional effort like this with remarkable ease, using your newsletter and additional mailings. As I suggested before, it's helpful to work every angle of a promotional campaign, so you would be wise to draw in the restaurant where your winners will dine for free. Do some stories on the restaurant. Ask them to have a little display somewhere regarding your contest. And when you choose the winning essay, have a photo taken of the child who won the contest, along with a story on how the child decided what to say about why his or her parents deserved the dinner out. If possible, get the photo and story into the local newspaper. And by all means, make sure that you put a story and photo into the newsletter that goes out to your target market.

Rand, Jill and I send a monthly newsletter to the clients, friends and potential clients for our newsletter service in which we offer thoughts about improving the effectiveness of one's marketing program. One of the most popular items is the monthly "Where Are We Now" Photo. Rand and Jill find a photo of themselves, me, our printers, members of the office staff and others as they enjoy a stop in some of their recent travels. (Enjoying your life, after all, is one of the constant themes we emphasize in our writings. That's a bit of preaching we're all willing to practice!) The actual place in the photo is never mentioned, so our readers are invited to send us the name of the place depicted in the photo. Correct entries are thrown in a hat, and a monthly winner is sent $25 to spend on lunch somewhere.

This is not a huge contest, obviously. No one's child will be sent to college with the $25 check, nor will it buy our client's next car. But it will buy a decent lunch, and the client has the satisfaction—for some, a bit of a thrill—of winning a contest.

Indeed, everyone wins…and no one has more fun with this than do Rand and Jill. Delightful conversations about shared experiences add depth to client relationships.

Contests that are initiated by your newsletter are a fabulous way to get people more aware of your marketing—and of you. A contest in which a great number of small (read: thoughtful, creative but relatively inexpensive) prizes are given out also provides you with a chance to contact more people in your target market.

Other Ideas

For several years, my real estate office rented an ice cream truck in the middle of the summer and drove up and down the streets of our target markets, handing out free popsicles. We preceded our "Free Popsicle Day" with flyers, mentioned it in newsletters, and had a flyer we handed out with each popsicle. The only problem we ran into was the occasional person who angrily demanded something other than a popsicle.

You'll also recall the moon cactus promotion I did early on. I also gave a piece of mistletoe to each home in my target market one holiday season. (I'll admit it: This was a huge piece of work, and more than one husband asked, chuckling, if I'd been kissing his wife. And if not, why not.) And I also put together packets of flower seeds for an early spring distribution. (Another hefty piece of work, but you can hire help…and people will never forget what you've done.)

I also spearheaded a number of community events. Looking back on it, I think I must have been somewhat out of my mind, but I also know these projects brought huge dividends. I initiated, with the help of others in the target market, a summer games weekend, with a 10K run, swimming races in a community pool, foot races and baseball games. Also with neighborhood help, I created a great haunted house in the community clubhouse for several Halloweens in a row. I also organized an Arts & Crafts Festival that took place the Saturday and Sunday after Thanksgiving, and community homeowners created booths from which they displayed and sold materials they had made over the year.

To take this to an even higher level, you might think of organizing a golf or tennis match, or a music festival, or a children's theater festival. This would be a major undertaking, and you would have to have a passion for what you're producing. But it could result in an annual event—a tradition that is associated with you—and bring you an endless stream of clients who love and appreciate what you have created.

When Do You Create Such "Amp-It-Up" Events?

A good time to do a minor- or medium-sized promotional event is early on in your marketing. This means that you will possibly want to do something—distribute moon cacti or mistletoe or whatever comes to your mind as an appropriate action—early in the process of sending out newsletters (or whatever the anchor of your marketing may be). It doesn't necessarily mean you're new to the business. If you've been in the business for five years but have never had a strong and consistent marketing program, you'll probably want to amp up people's awareness of you and your marketing program in the first few months of operating that program.

A major "amp-it-up" event—a sports tournament, a musical festival or concert, a color-the-Thanksgiving-turkey contest for the kids—should be an annual affair. Ideally, it will come around faithfully and consistently every year. People will be able to rely on it, will look forward to it, will consider it a constant part of their community's life.

I would be remiss, I think, if I left this subject without adding a few words of caution. The bottom line is that your "amp-it-up" events should arise from your own interests and passions. If you have a passion for folk music, for example, what could be better than to produce a summer weekend of folk music in the city park? It's a huge piece of work, but it can be extremely rewarding. You get to interact with some of your favorite musicians, pull together an enthusiastic audience of fellow music lovers, and create something good for your community.

What comes to mind, however, is an annual "amp-it-up" effort by a real estate professional I used to know vaguely. This didn't involve her passion, didn't give people a better idea of who she was and what she loved—it was just an annual giveaway. Every year, she contracted to buy a few truckloads of pumpkins from a relative and she passed out free pumpkins before Halloween in her target market ("farm").

This sounds, on the surface, like a pretty wonderful idea, and it did indeed make people aware of who she was very quickly. So far, so good.

But she became known as "the Pumpkin Lady." She totally lacked follow-through, didn't maximize her promotional effort, didn't take it to completion.

A good friend of mine who worked for another real estate company and had taken on this lady's "farm" area, demonstrated what was lacking in the Pumpkin Lady's annual giveaway. When Pumpkin Lady distributed her pumpkins throughout the target market, my friend sent around flyers inviting everyone to a pumpkin-carving picnic in a local park. Dozens of homeowners brought their children. My friend supplied refreshments, special (safe) pumpkin-carving knives, trash bags, and several adults to help with the whole affair. When all the pumpkins had been carved, everyone voted on the best and most artistic Jack-o-lanterns, and my friend supplied a lot of small prizes.

Everyone went home happy. My friend (who was never called the Pumpkin Guy) continued his energetic, creative approach to marketing, and he soon owned the target market, taking far more listings there than anyone else in the business.

Giving out pumpkins once a year cannot be the anchor of your marketing program. It can only be an effort that amps up what you're already doing and what you will continue to do consistently. And when you dive into an "amp-it-up" project, be sure to think through all aspects of the task and every way that people can benefit from and enjoy it. There would be no harm in being known as the "folk music real estate guy" but, if your monthly marketing program is working for you, it's far more likely that you'd be known as "the real estate guy behind that great folk music festival."

PART THREE

Promise And Experience

CHAPTER FOURTEEN

What Kind of Experience Does Your Marketing Promise

The operative marketing term here is "promise."

What is your promise as a real estate professional? That is, what can you assure potential clients they will experience if they choose to work with you? It's about *their* experience, not about *your* qualities and character—though their experience will be better precisely because of all that you bring to it as their real estate professional.

It's a bit subtle, but stay with me on this.

Based on the kind of marketing program we have been looking at, you can promise extremely good service. You can promise knowledge and experience. You can promise energy and commitment. You can promise consistency. You can promise a trustworthy relationship. You can promise a real estate professional who operates on values that the client is at home with. You can promise...what? A safe, solid, profitable transaction? An experience that is—surprise!—actually more fun than not.

What is crucial here, again, is that you aren't so much promising aspects of yourself as you are promising aspects of the buyer's and seller's experience of you. You are, in an almost subconscious way, creating a contract with a potential buyer or seller in which you promise to deliver a particular kind of experience, filled with the desirable qualities that the buyer or seller wants.

There are few things more potent than having a sense of promise that is clear and credible to current and potential clients. Everyone is on the same page of music, working in harmony, enjoying the process, confident about the outcome. Let's look at a couple of examples of "promise" at work.

Windham Hill Records

You may or may not recall when Will Ackerman was first releasing music on his own Windham Hill Record label. He began with a recording of his own, elegantly spare, exquisitely recorded solo guitar pieces. (Then he drove from record store to record store with boxes of his album—this was before CDs had been invented—in the back seat of his car.)

There was great consistency to the early Windham Hill recordings. The album covers, with their bold use of white space and exquisite nature photographs (generally taken by Ackerman's wife), let you know immediately that you were holding a Windham Hill record in your hands. And the sound was similar—in the sense that all the musicians worked in a gentle, minimalist style that came to be known as part of the New Age Music movement. If you liked a Windham Hill recording, you could pick up any other Windham Hill recording and the chances were extremely strong that you would like that as well.

What could be better for the record label? Windham Hill built up a very loyal following, became known as the innovator in a gentle, rewarding kind of instrumental music, and sold a lot of recordings. Inevitably, they were copied by several other such record labels, but they paved the way.

Though they still exist (in spite of Ackerman's departure), the "Windham Hill sound" went by the wayside as they expanded the range of styles that they recorded and offered. They had faced a difficult Catch-22, a point in their growth where, to continue expanding, they would have to range out into other styles of music. They opted for growth and lost a great deal in the process. Now you can find contemporary jazz releases, modern folk music, Hawaiian slack-key guitar and other styles under the Windham Hill banner. You can also sense a degree of integrity to this music, whatever the style, but you don't have the confident expectation—as you may have had in the past—that the music will fit your personal taste.

Still, the Windham Hill story stands as a great example of promise in marketing.

Trader Joe's Markets

I'm fortunate to have known the quirky genius who created Trader Joe's, Joe Coulombe, and to have studied his thinking first-hand. It was from Joe that I first heard the term, "promise," learned about carefully limiting the range of what you offer, saw the importance of consistency in marketing and began to understand how crucial the sense of experience is.

Very early on, Joe was working with my father at a large retail drug store chain when the two of them tried to engineer a leveraged buy-out of one of the company's smaller chains of stores, Owl Drugs. Both of these men were furiously ambitious and wanted to own their own shops and trusted one another enough to do so in partnership. When the buy-out fizzled (the first time I ever heard my father repeat certain unprintable comments deep into the night), my Dad went to work for Lucky Stores, running their Gemco discount department stores. Joe, on the other hand, bought a small chain of Southern California convenience markets.

Gradually, Joe transformed these little markets—which sold cigarettes, pop, beer and candy (and "whose promise," Joe later admitted, was "physical and emotional suicide for the customer")— into unique specialty gourmet shops. To my eyes, what he was doing was to create shops that sold his favorite things (fine wines, cheeses, imported sweets, innovative gourmet and health-oriented products) at the lowest possible prices. To his eyes, he was responding to the many people who had traveled abroad and developed a wider array of tastes in foods than could be satisfied at the local supermarket. Little did even Joe know how many people fit into his client profile.

Joe began by throwing out cigarettes. His competitors told him he was crazy. Then he threw out Coke, in part because they operated with such a heavy hand in his store. His competitors suggested they might start up a charity fund to make sure he could close his shops gracefully.

Everything he removed from his stores he replaced with products that attracted a large number of eager buyers. He said his ideal customer was a former Rhodes Scholar who had been to Europe, had developed expensive tastes in foods and other products and now could no longer find or afford those products. His brilliant specialty was to find those products in quantities smaller than the major chains could handle, and then to offer the vendor pennies on the dollar to take the product off his hands. He and his growing staff of experts could taste a sample of a small available quantity of wine and, if it was up to their standards, they bought it up cheaply and passed most of the savings on to their customers.

Their marketing program? Joe created a nearly absurd little 16-page flyer using very old woodcuts for illustrations and dropping in corny captions, a veritable feast of bad puns, and explained a large number of the products he was currently offering. Maybe he'd wangled a small-sized load of a kind of cheese you'd never heard of before. He'd explain it, how it's made, where it's made, why it's tasty, what it's good with, and how he could offer it at such a good price. You'd go into the store with your copy of the month's "Fearless Flyer" and ask for some of the cheese. Simple as that.

So far, what we have here is masterful, inexpensive Information Marketing—very like what can be done by real estate professionals in their own newsletters (and in newspaper columns as well as on the Internet). It is hugely effective. It isn't about how wonderful Trader Joe's stores are; it's about the experience you'll have in the stores and very specific reasons for shopping there.

After you have a few good experiences in the local Trader Joe's store, you do three things: First, you continue trying new things offered by the store, having come to believe the promise that everything in the store will be of high quality and sell at low prices (though, of course, you may find that soy taco chips and tapanade, as two examples, aren't to your own liking). There is a sense of discovery in the Trader Joe's promise, a sense of value, good health, people who are enthusiastic about what they're putting on the store shelves for you to buy and are always ready to help you.

So the second thing you are likely to do is to tell your friends and family – and not just that the store exists. Soon you are racing to tell one another about products you've found and liked. "Try the green chile sauce! And, oh! That frozen key lime pie! It's to die for!" One loyal shopper made this enthusiastic declaration in the *New York Times* article welcoming Trader Joe's to New York City: "This sounds crazy, but you feel like the company likes food even more than they like money. You don't feel that at the supermarket."

And this, too, is precisely the kind of response you want to your own marketing and–please notice–it demonstrates the way you fulfill what you are putting out there in your marketing. By fulfilling your constant promises, both overt and implied. If you promise good products, always tasty, always healthy, then that's exactly what you must provide.

Trader Joe's is still going strong and growing successfully. It was bought by a German food chain which had the wisdom to leave it alone, for the most part, and to support all that had gone right with the stores. Joe Coulombe, though, left the company in 1989.

One last thing. My Dad, who is now deceased, went on to be president and CEO of the massive Lucky Stores food market chain. He and Joe talked with one another on a monthly basis, sharing experiences, trying out new ideas. Not that long before retiring, Dad sent a formal offer for Lucky Stores to purchase Trader Joe's. Joe wrote back, thanking him for the confidence he had shown in the company. However, he said, a big corporation like Lucky Stores would ruin a concept like Trader Joe's very quickly. He couldn't allow that to happen to his company and the employees who had dedicated their careers to it.

Dad understood. I imagine most of my readers understand, too. (The point has great relevance to the advantage you have in personal marketing, as a unique real estate professional, over the office or corporation where your license hangs. For one thing, the corporation can't market itself to a specific segment of the marketplace. You can!)

A Company Of One

One of your strengths as a real estate professional is that you are virtually a company unto yourself. You can create your own marketing program and do business in your own way. Unlike a corporation, which is forced to say its personnel all act in a certain way–even when they don't–you can be very detailed about the experience your clients have of you and of their purchase and sale of real estate. It's your promise, not a generalized piece of nonsense that somehow has to speak for a diverse bunch of real estate professionals.

This is one of the reasons that advertising by major brokerage firms tends to be so lame and ineffectual. Television ads, especially, are a tremendous waste of money (though a few real estate professionals have pointed out to me that their main purpose is to attract new real estate agents to the company. If that is true, it has to be more expensive than effectual). The work and marketing of the individual real estate professional is where the rubber really meets the road. Never forget that.

So you are uniquely positioned to create your own very successful marketing program and a career that reflects who you are, not who some PR guy at the corporate office believes you should be portrayed to be.

CHAPTER FIFTEEN
Putting Promise into Words

The first thing that comes to mind regarding an advertisement about your promise may be some car dealer on late night television hawking his dealership and the cars they're currently offering. "Hey! I'm Mal Blythington, and I'll stand on my head to make you a deal!"

This kind of nonsense is about nothing more than getting your attention. Nearly everyone is aware that ol' Mal would far rather stand on *their* heads to make them a deal. The promise offered by this auto dealership was not a pleasant one. "Come on down to Manipulation City and let us throw your keys on the roof while you test drive one of our vehicles!"

Quite understandably, most people in our society have come to associate advertising and marketing with aggravation and deception. Further, they have come to assume that advertising must aggravate and deceive in order to be effective. But Americans have long ago become rather immune to this sort of marketing.

A fine marketing guru, Seth Godin, calls this "Interruption Marketing" and notes that it just doesn't work any more. He's doubtless right.

When Joe Coulombe finally got around to spending a bit more on his marketing, he put ads on the radio that explained, in a simple, interesting and straightforward way, the qualities of a certain product the store was featuring and the reason for its price. For example, one ad explained why fish that is frozen at sea is even healthier and, in many respects, even fresher and tastier than what is generally known as "fresh" fish.

What if homes were marketed in this fashion? No, not frozen at sea and marketed as fresh. But marketed through what might be called Deep Informational Marketing.

What if, instead of leaving out crucial information so that people will call with questions…what if the information were delivered in a friendly, candid, detailed fashion? It wouldn't aim to grab people's attention in order to manipulate them into dialing you up on the phone. And it wouldn't begin your relationship with potential clients by saying, in effect, "My promise is that I will manipulate and deceive you so that I can earn a commission." Not a good promise to be sending out into the world.

Unfortunately, many people expect that negative promise. They *don't* expect an experience that is a great deal safer, more gratifying, less tense, more helpful than that. Give them reason to expect a better, more humane, more mature experience—and you are likely to attract a very strong clientele.

But how do you give them reason to expect better than the old bait-and-switch? We've talked about the importance of always providing service—through your newsletters, through your advertising, through your newspaper columns, through whatever you choose to do in your marketing program. Let's look now at the core elements, the most basic parts of your marketing program that identify you and that stand behind everything you do and further, that clients and potential clients can and will refer to when they think of or describe the experience they have of a transaction with you.

Let's look at:

1. Your basic slogan(s),

2. Your logo,

3. Your mission statement,

4. And your transaction "script."

CHAPTER SIXTEEN
Your Slogan

A couple of decades ago, especially in out-of-the-way urban areas, it seemed that the most widely-used slogan could easily be found somewhere in a real estate shop's windows. Printed in large letters on a piece of cardboard were three words: "We need listings!" The intent here, of course, was NOT to tell people that the business was desperate and needed listings if it was to survive, though that may have been the first thing that pops into your head when you read it. The intended implication was that this real estate office was working with so darn many enthusiastic buyers that it had a severe shortage of listings to show them. Hey—list with us and we'll sell your home to one of our many buyers, pronto! Honest!

It's a dreadful slogan, of course, but it's instructive to notice why it's so dreadful. For one thing, it's very open to negative interpretation, as we've just seen. For another, it's about the real estate company, not about buyers or sellers who might work with the company. And what is the promise wrapped up in this slogan? It's that you can be confident you'll experience being lied to by these people…because their slogan is, at best, a manipulative fabrication. Sadly, this used to be a listing technique: The promise of bringing buyers to your house IF you list with me.

So—let's look for the following three qualities in a slogan.

Does it…

▶ 1. Display clarity of meaning (and a concise use of words),

▶ 2. Talk about clients' needs and wishes, not about the qualities or needs of the company or of the individual agent, and

▶ 3. Convey a positive promise of what clients can expect to experience from this company or individual agent?

With these qualifying questions in mind, let's look at some slogans I've seen.

Slogan: George Reynolds...
"The multi-million dollar producer."

Comments: There are dozens of variations on this, of course, especially now that it's possible for real estate professionals in high-price areas to become multi-million dollar producers by simply selling one house.

The beauty of this slogan is the way it plays into the advice of many authors in books about how to buy or sell a home: Find the agents who are doing the most business, the authors suggest. They're probably the ones who know how to get the job done.

Okay. I guess. But does someone who is a member of the Silver Turnip Producer Club have your best interests at heart? Will you find yourself compatible with this person? Will this person be at least as interested in helping you fulfill your needs and wishes as he or she is in becoming a still-larger producer and buying a yet-fancier automobile?

The fact is, this sort of slogan is old stuff. Here's why:

▶ 1. Clarity of meaning: Yes, it's clear, but what does it have to do with me, the potential client, and my experience of the contemplated transaction?

▶ 2. Talks about client: No. It talks about the salesperson. At best, the potential client may pick up the implication that the salesperson is successful and therefore, in theory, is a good person to work with.

▶ 3. Promise: The promise here is rather dreadful. This slogan strips the deal down to dollars—the salesperson's dollars, not the client's dollars. The likely promise, therefore, is that clients will feel like the salesperson's next meal ticket.

Slogan: Robert Dawkins...
"A house-sold word."

Comments: Because this is a rather witty pun (or at least, it was the first time we saw it), there was the likelihood that it would both capture the attention of potential clients and cause them to think for a moment. But was it just witty, or did it work?

▶ 1. Clarity of meaning: The meaning, actually, isn't all that clear.

Robert is apparently known well enough to be a household word. Further, he is known for selling houses and, presumably, for doing it well. Good enough, I suppose.

▶ 2. Talks about client: Not really. There is the implication that the client will benefit because Robert really does get houses sold. But that's as far as it goes.

▶ 3. Promise: The promise, actually, is rather clear. Robert will get your house sold. Will it be a good experience, a profitable experience, a terrible experience? Who knows?

But at least Robert got the attention of those who haven't seen this slogan enough times to overlook it instantly, as well as those who are still saying things like, "I resemble that remark," for the six thousandth time and finding it funny.

Slogan: Ted Paulino...
"Expert in home delivery."

Comment: I rather like this, perhaps because I haven't seen it much. It's another witty pun, but it can backfire occasionally.

▶ 1. Clarity of meaning: The meaning is fairly clear. It seems to say, "I know how to get you into (or out of) a home" and "I deliver."

▶ 2. Talks about client: No. This talks about the agent, not the client.

▶ 3. Promise: "Home delivery" is both a clever and a dangerous phrase. It has a sweetness to it, since it conjures up a sense of a baby being delivered. On the other hand, other than to suggest his backing for the ideals of home and the family, Mr. Paulino here is edging into very personal territory. Not all memories of childbirth are wonderful. Not all homes will have babies in them. And there is the slightly scary possibility that people will sense a relationship between the real estate transaction and the process of a home birth.

Above all, though, what does this tell us about how our experience of a transaction with Mr. Paulino will be?

Slogan: Roberta Wayland...
"I work where I live." (or I live where I work).

Comments: What comes to my mind immediately, I must admit, is the old saying about how certain animals won't foul their own nests. Still, the meaning here is generally positive.

▶ 1. Clarity of meaning: This is prosaic, but the sentence is self-explanatory at a very basic level. So obvious is it that it tends to make you wonder if there are hidden meanings here. So the impact isn't as sharp as it could be.

▶ 2. Talks about clients: Well, no...it talks about the agent, who lives in the neighborhood where she works. The benefit for clients—at least, for those who live in the neighborhood or move into it—is fairly clear. She is knowledgeable about the area. She will want to maintain the neighborhood's quality of life.

▶ 3. Promise: So our agent (who was, in real life, an extraordinarily successful real estate professional) will treat us like esteemed neighbors and will watch out for the neighborhood. She seems to say: We're in this together, the similarity of our social/economic makeup is implicit; and I'm an expert in the qualities of this area.

Okay. There is, among other things, something of an integrity issue being communicated here. But what, really, is my experience going to be like if I work with this person?

Slogan: Sunny Fields...
"Sustainable real estate
for a sustainable community."

Comments: Understand that many people in the marketplace won't even understand the meaning of the words here. But others most definitely will. And if they are concerned about environmental issues and take those concerns into the way they live, the kind of home they choose, the lifestyle they prefer, they will be very attracted to this slogan.

▶ 1. Clarity of meaning: As I just suggested, this won't be clear to everyone in town. It may even be slightly offensive to some because the word "sustainable" has become a negative code word to them. However, it will be very clear to those who cherish environmental concerns and are committed to a sustainable lifestyle.

▶ 2. Talks about client: While this doesn't describe the client, it does speak directly to the concerns of a broad group of potential clients, and doesn't seek to tell us who the real estate professional is, but rather to show us.

▶ 3. Promise: The promise here is crucial. This will be an experience that is in integrity with many potential clients' deeply-felt beliefs and commitments. There is the further promise that a certain lifestyle will result — characterized by simplicity, by authenticity, even by organic and natural features in the home.

Obviously, such a slogan only works for someone who is herself committed to the values of sustainability. But that's just the point. Your slogan must be absolutely true about you, conveying the promise of the kind of experience your clients can look forward to in working with you.

How To Create A Slogan

Creating a slogan is a difficult, but potentially revealing, experience. How in the world can you narrow down the heart and soul of your promise into a few, succinct words?

Step one (Remember Marketing Principle #2: Know Thyself) is to get very clear about how you will "position" yourself in the market. Who are the people who will get the most from your service? Who, therefore, are the people you will concentrate on marketing yourself to? Who are the people, in short, who make up your target market?

Then, I suggest you sit down with family, then with friends, then with business associates. Ask them who you are, how you interact with people, what seems to matter the most to you. Take it all in. Write it all down.

Then ask each group of friends, family and associates how they would distill the experience of doing something with you into one or two sentences. Take it all in and write it all down.

Then spend time alone, preferably when you won't be disturbed. Think about the target market you will be marketing your promise to. What kind of people are they? In what ways are they distinctly similar to you?

Think, too, about exactly how you would want to be treated by a real estate professional. Think of the ideal professional, how he or she treats you, what it is like to communicate with him or her, how he or she gets the job done, how he or she communicates with you throughout every stage of the transaction, how he or she treats you when the deal closes, and how he or she remains in contact with you after all is said and done.

That's you. That's the experience you promise to deliver.

What is the essence of that experience? Undeniably, I'm asking about the essence of who you are in the world. Gulp.

Start playing with phrases:

Bill Fisher...*bringing your dreams to life*

Bill Fisher...*making it all possible*

Bill Fisher...*helping you bring it all home*

Bill Fisher...*the experience, energy and information you need*

Bill Fisher...*your family home is your greatest investment*

Bill Fisher...*home becomes sanctuary*

Bill Fisher...*daring to dream, making it real*

Bill Fisher...*your own wishes and goals find their home*

What To Do With Your Slogan

I may or may not have moved in the direction of a slogan that you can adapt for your own use. I'll repeat: The slogan should distill who you are and how you treat people and like being treated yourself and, crucially, your slogan should reflect the most deeply-held values of your target market.

You will be married to this slogan (though you can change it whenever you wish, but as seldom as possible and, ideally, never). Choose carefully. Find words that carry an unusual beauty for you, a positive energy, a piece of who you are.

And put the slogan everywhere. On your business cards, on your marketing materials, on your advertising, on your website, on your stationery. As I said, you may someday choose to change your slogan, so you won't want to apply it to your body in a tattoo. But people should see it nearly as often as they see your face.

You'll find, then, that when you introduce yourself to a stranger, he or she will very often say, "Ah, yes. 'Daring to dream, making it real.'"

"Yes," you can say. "The very one."

CHAPTER SEVENTEEN
Mission Statement

Most businesses—and, as I've said before, you are a business (among other things)—develop a business plan and a mission statement. You will benefit from doing the same.

Your business plan is slightly beyond the purview of this book. What I do want to say, though, is that it is extremely helpful to know approximately how much income you want to earn (that is, how much you will be earning), approximately how many transactions it will take to bring in that much income, and how, generally, you plan to generate that business.

A brief digression: For many people in the real estate professions, there comes the realization after a while that—good grief!—I can earn a lot of money at this job...far more than I ever imagined earning! At this point, there is a temptation to throw the business plan to the sharks and simply go for as much income as possible, whatever that turns out to be. This is a recipe for burning out.

A crucial element, right at the top of your business plan, is that your business must support your whole life. It must not become your whole life, and it must not, as Roger Bannister suggested about his sport, run your life. You are not a house. You are not your job. Your job is not you. You are a varied, complex, creative person with a life to match. If you remember this priority when you reach the realization that there's more money to be made here than you imagined, you may adjust your income goal a bit higher, but don't take it a lot higher than the amount of money you need to live a good and satisfying life. It is inestimably important that you do, indeed, live that life.

A simple principle: You are paid in the money from your commissions and/or salary, in the satisfaction of giving needed assistance to people and bringing value into their lives, and in the time and ability to be with your family, friends, associates and hobbies. Do not shortchange yourself in any of these categories. The desire to step into the Louvre Museum and take your own look at a few of the works of Leonardo da

Vinci , for example, is no small thing. If that is high on your list, give it to yourself. Pay yourself with it. The same, of course, is to be said for the ability to attend your son's and daughter's baseball games and piano recitals.

Your Mission Statement

I was part of a task force that put together the mission statement for our church several years ago, and I was amazed at how much work went into the project. It was a bit like making maple syrup – taking initial materials, boiling them down, boiling them down, and then boiling them down some more, then putting those materials with others and starting the boiling process yet again.

It took pages and pages of notes, dozens of them, to come up with about six sentences, and we learned a vast amount about the church we wanted, about our sense of purpose and about ourselves in the process.

Why Create A Mission Statement?

Several reasons:

▶ 1. As with your slogan, but in a more fully-developed way, you are distilling who you are and what you are about as a real estate professional.

▶ 2. You are creating a fuller statement of your promise, one that you and your clients can refer to, one that you can judge your performance against.

▶ 3. You are placing yourself and your actions in the real world and determining the ways in which you are a positive force, promoting all you most truly believe in.

I suggest you approach the mission statement after you have developed your slogan. You will have gone through a lengthy look at how you see yourself, how others see you, and who you want to be in your profession. The material for your mission statement should be close at hand already.

I would also suggest that you won't be as married to your mission statement as you will to your slogan because, as your career develops and you experience the range of activities you can involve yourself in and the good you can do, you will likely want to revise your mission statement in an even more positive and comprehensive direction.

Unlike your slogan, your mission statement won't go out in every mailing, in every advertisement, on every business card. It's more of a time-release capsule that you look at every now and then, and check how closely aligned it still is to your business and personal practices. You may want to put it into your listing presentation, into your client kit (for buyers), framed on or above your desk, and perhaps laminated and attached in your car (inside, not flapping in the wind). It should be a statement that fills you with pride, that inspires you, that makes you bigger than you thought you were. It should be something you strive hard to live up to.

Sample Mission Statements

Here is the mission statement developed by the innovative health and beauty products company, Aveda:

> *Our mission at Aveda is to care for the world we live in, from the products we make to the ways in which we give back to society. At Aveda, we strive to set an example for environmental leadership and responsibility, not just in the world of beauty, but around the world.*

As with any good mission statement, this is difficult to criticize. In fact, why try? Indeed, perhaps one of the best indications that a mission statement is doing its job is this reaction: "I have no reason to want to criticize this. In fact, I'd like to be a part of it."

Let's take a look, though, at the mission statement published for Trader Joe's. It is homey, honest…but it rambles a bit:

> *At Trader Joe's, our mission is to bring our customers the best food and beverage values and the information to make informed buying decisions. There are more than 2000 unique grocery items in our label, all at honest everyday low prices. We work hard at buying things right: Our buyers travel the world searching for new items and we work with a variety of suppliers who make interesting products for us, many of them exclusive to Trader Joe's. All our private label products have their own "angle," i.e., vegetarian, Kosher, organic or just plain decadent, and all have minimally processed ingredients.*

Obviously, this isn't intended to be a pithy statement of what Trader

Joe's is all about, though a great deal is packed into this paragraph. Instead, it's the beginning of a longer statement titled, "The Story of Trader Joe's." As with all of the Trader Joe's information marketing material, it is fun, unpretentious, very informative and rather iconoclastic. It doesn't sound like a bunch of PR elves sat up late at night developing slick verbiage. It sounds like one of the store managers knocked it off rather quickly…because he knows exactly what Trader Joe's is about.

If you research mission statements, you will probably find that most are far too long and lofty and general. They remind me of the wonderful story involving actor and comedian Danny Kaye. He was attending a wedding, and the ceremony was filled with readings of poetry, Grateful Dead lyrics, advice from Kahlil Gibran. Finally, in exasperation, Kaye yelled out from a middle pew, "Get on with it!"

This is not the way you want people to react to your mission statement. You want it to be genuine, clear, totally relevant and true. And you want to cut to the chase from the very first words. Note, for example, this mission statement from *iSanDiegoRealEstate.com*, an information real estate website assembled by Realty Executives:

> *Committed to providing clients with the highest quality service and attention, being sensitive to their needs and dedicated to their satisfaction, aggressively and enthusiastically striving to achieve their best interests, treating them fairly, with honesty, courtesy and professionalism.*

With these rather lofty ideals in mind, I will run the following up the flagpole and see if anyone salutes. It's a mission statement for my own marketing/newsletter business:

> *The success of my business is measured by the quantity and especially the quality of my clients' business transactions and careers. Those, in turn, are measured by how well the marketing materials I create inform and assist the clients and potential clients of my own clients in the real estate professions, and how well my own clients' best qualities and abilities are represented by my work. My writings help guide the public through the intricacies of real estate and related personal finance questions, adding value to all aspects of their lives and supporting the quality of life in their communities.*

As you can see, it is as if I'm sailing and I know exactly what my destination is. My mission statement is like the distant lighthouse I continually aim at, constantly correcting the direction my tiller is taking me. It is, in short, the ideal of my business. Needless to say, I will—I must—always strive to make it completely accurate and true.

Still—there is something missing here. Indeed, according to my own biases, there is something missing from even the best mission statements I have seen. They tell. They don't show. And so they do indeed sound lofty, perhaps without their feet on the ground, and very likely unattached in any obvious way to the person or business that wrote the statement.

What to do? **Create a story or stories.** Which is another way of saying: Show, don't tell.

Let's reconsider the concept of the mission statement, therefore, and think of it as a dynamic job application. Instead of telling someone all your highest ideals, you endeavor to provide someone a meaningful experience of who you are in your professional life.

Example:

Bob Bryson and his partner Clark Smith hung their new company sign in front of their newly-established office about twenty-five years ago in Laguna Beach. They needed to create a presence in their local marketplace, so they placed a weekly full-page advertisement in "The Pennysaver," then commonly accepted as the prime source of real estate information. After a year, they assessed how well their ads were doing for them and found they could only trace one transaction (with a $5,000 commission) to their advertising (which had cost them roughly $40,000 over the course of the year).

They decided to stop advertising altogether. Instead, they began to send out one of the newsletters I create every month. This must be informative, valuable, and sophisticated, they said. That's the nature of the client we want to attract.

Over twenty years later, Bryson told me that their business had constantly grown and they'd both made a great deal of money. Even more important, they've loved it. Their relationship with their clients has been almost uniformly excellent. Now, over 90% of their business is repeat and referral. They still get calls for advice and consultation from newsletter recipients whom they have never met. They have always been in the business for the long haul, and have offered their real estate knowledge freely. And their only advertising all these years, other than word of mouth, has been the newsletter.

"Our motto," declares Bryson, "is 'Hold the Course'—because we know after more than twenty years that it works."

The success of my marketing business is measured by the quantity and especially the quality of both the transactions and the careers of people like Bryson and Smith. That success, further, is measured by how well the marketing materials I create inform and assist their clients and potential clients, and how well my own clients' best qualities and abilities are represented by my work. To that end, my writings help guide the public through the intricacies of real estate and related personal finance questions, adding value to all aspects of their lives and supporting the quality of life in the communities in which they reside.

CHAPTER EIGHTEEN
Your Logo

Alogo is essentially a visual counterpart to a slogan. It doesn't necessarily have to say the same thing that the slogan says. Indeed, it can work like a second slogan.

When I was working as "The Village San Juan Specialist" in a development with the same name, I chose a little drawing by the wonderful E. H. Shephard of Christopher Robin walking with a fishing pole over his shoulder. (A few words about copyright issues in a moment.) Because it was obviously a little boy and, to many, very identifiable–carrying with it the good feelings of *Winnie-the-Pooh*, and because I was a hard-working real estate guy, I had no trouble with people saying, "Ah, you'd rather be fishing than working on my transaction, eh?" It was just a friendly, light-hearted way of bringing to mind the funky lake at the entrance to Village San Juan.

I wouldn't use it again for two reasons.

1. I don't really like to fish. If I did like to fish, and if I were producing an annual fishing derby for children (and, perhaps, adults), the little logo might have made more sense. But hey, what did I know in 1976?

2. The copyright issue. Anything connected to *Winnie-the-Pooh*, including the great old E. H. Shephard drawings, is owned and copyrighted by Disney now. If you're one real estate professional in one little area using one little drawing, don't expect leniency from the Disney Corporation. In short, don't use copyrighted artwork (unless you get written permission).

What Constitutes A Logo?

I'm using the term very loosely here. It could be a simple piece of artwork, a face, a cartoon, a scene that brings your target market to mind, any other image that evokes the values or experiences of your target market, or a stylized reworking of your name or slogan or both.

Personally, I very much like a representative little bit of artwork, and I suggest you have a true-blue artist, ideally a professional, sit down with you, get an idea of what you're after, and draw up a few options for you. This person could be an artistic stepson, by the way, as would be the case for me, or could be a graphic artist recommended by a friend. But be careful about asking a friend or relative who has no experience in graphic arts.

When I sought a logo for my real estate company (The Orange Valley Real Estate Company in San Juan Capistrano), I turned to a graphic artist who was a good friend of one of my top agents. He came up with several designs, one of which simply knocked me out, two stylized oranges with three stylized leaves. He wasn't as pleased with it as I was, but he worked with me, refined it a bit, and soon we had some of the most exquisite 'For Sale' signs in the nation. Or so I thought.

Sound easy? It wasn't. It was a hellish process, in fact. Before turning to Paul, who designed our beautiful logo, I had gone with a company that promised one drawing that they knew I would accept. The result was very heavy on orange and black and looked like a directional sign for a Halloween party to me. The rep from the design company was utterly astonished at my reaction, implying that I didn't know what I was talking about and had no taste and should accept the design because it would win awards. It won no awards from me.

For a month, we tried to come up with our own designs, we called upon friends, upon children, upon wives of business associates. We had to reject dozens of designs, which is about as fun as having wisdom teeth removed, and we paid fees to people for the time they had put in. On and on it went, so that when Paul came up with the design we loved, we treated him as a conquering hero.

Do not, in short, expect the logo process to be any easier than the slogan process. In fact, it will almost certainly be harder. But keep in mind the benefits of having an identifiable logo that has good connotations for people. Our stylized oranges and three leaves with pleasing brown lettering and a white background won a great deal of praise from the community and very soon was as recognizable to most residents as, well, a picture of Colonel Sanders perhaps.

A logo will not bring you business, obviously. It is not the basis or foundation of your marketing program, but it is tremendously helpful to have your name, your photograph, your slogan, and your logo—all identifying you, all reminding people of you, all inspiring good thoughts. All over the place.

CHAPTER NINETEEN

The Ideal Transaction

There is another carefully-constructed statement that you will want to work on. This is a script, in essence, and you needn't show it to anyone—just keep it firmly in your mind...always.

Before we get to it, let's look at an important question: The reader may have stayed with me enthusiastically through parts one and two of this book, but it's possible that a few of you started to nod off during part three, primarily because you really don't want to go to the trouble of creating a slogan, mission statement and logo.

Guess what. You don't have to. Your career doesn't depend on it.

But you will gain immensely from doing so.

This last thing, though—the visualizing of your ideal transaction— is a required assignment. It will help you remember that you aren't working with (as my old friend worded it) "assholes." It will help you empathize with those you are serving. And it will make certain that everything you do in a transaction leads to a specific goal (and it's not just the commission): The creation and/or nourishment of a richly successful career.

What does that mean? Let's take a look.

▶ 1. A potential client calls, saying she has been reading your newsletter for several months and happened to meet you once at the market. She feels she already knows you from the materials you send out, so it was easy to call on you for help in selling her home.

This is a warm client. She and her husband already have a degree of trust in you and are open to what you may suggest. It will be easy to develop a constructive relationship, built on solid, empathic communication, very quickly. (You will obviously have a very slightly different script for your transactions with buyers.)

▶ 2. You arrive at their home that evening to find out exactly what they wish to accomplish, to look at the property, to show them a competitive market analysis, and to determine what should happen next. By the end of the evening, you are completely in tune with their needs and wishes, you have gotten to know their property, they are satisfied that they've developed an asking price that is justified by actual market conditions, and they know exactly the steps you will be taking to market their home.

Needless to say, it is crucial that you communicate often with your new clients, letting them know what is happening in the marketing of the home, how agents and potential buyers are responding to the home, what further steps might be taken, and what is happening in the overall market. It would also be good to take a bit of time to rehearse how an offer will be heard, especially if market conditions are extraordinary. (There is a wonderful term in child-raising: foreshadowing. If you let people know what to expect and what to do when the expected—and especially the unexpected—take place, they roll with the changes far more gracefully.)

▶ 3. An offer is accepted. You watch over the closing process with great care, keeping the clients informed about what is happening and when it will happen.

▶ 4. The transaction closes. You bring your clients a gourmet eat-it-with-your-fingers meal to consume during the day of moving. You provide any last-minute help that may be needed.

▶ 5. By now you have a great deal of information about these clients. You know the children, their ages, their birthdays, their expected dates of graduation. You know the birthdays of the homeowners, when they married. You have plenty of info for birthday and anniversary cards, and you know when you'll want to call and ask about a child's graduation, what he or she will be doing next, and other aspects of everyone's life. You do this, frankly, because you have come to care about these people—not just because you want more business.

Meanwhile, you have been sending a newsletter to this client every month, along with any other marketing materials you may be generating. You continue to keep people informed about real estate matters, long after the transaction has closed. Why? Because every truly satisfied client is a new-client-generator, very likely to send you relatives, friends, and associates who need your help with their real estate transactions.

Remember the Trader Joe's story? People love to be the one who helps their friends discover Trader Joe's and to talk about specific products the store offers. On a recent visit to Trader Joe's, I overheard two elderly women pondering which brand of a particular product to buy. Another shopper, a much younger woman, rushed around from the next aisle and suggested they try the frozen version of the product. Soon, they were talking and laughing and discovering that the younger woman's best friend was the youngest niece of one of the elderly women.

People, similarly, will take great pride and pleasure in telling their friends and family and associates about you, about the quality of service they can expect from you, about the wonderful experience of working with you and getting to know you. And if they're receiving your marketing materials, they'll also call friends and family and associates to tell them of some of the valuable information you're sharing.

It is impossible to overemphasize the importance of past clients as the core of your target market. Consider this because it is difficult to believe: **Most real estate professionals, astonishingly, simply let people disappear once a deal is done.** This is like abandoning a gold mine after finding the first nugget. Every transaction should lead to at least a dozen future transactions, probably more and, indirectly, a great many more than that. This is the foundation of your career in real estate.

The ideal real estate transaction, therefore, builds upon the success of your marketing program to create positive experiences in successful transactions and warm, meaningful client relationships that last a lifetime and continue to generate business as long as you are in real estate. It also embodies a guiding principle in your career:

Service-Oriented Marketing Principle #21:
All of your business is generated by
all that you do.

In real estate, as in many other fields, you are actually always marketing the experience that you provide as a real estate or mortgage professional...and as a caring human being.

PART FOUR

The Newsletter & Other Parts
Of Your Marketing Program

CHAPTER TWENTY
The Target Market Database

O kay, time to dive into it. Having done all the self-examination described in the first several chapters and having decided upon a slogan, a mission statement, a logo and the script for your ideal transaction, it's time to start building your actual marketing program.

Step One: Setting Up Your Target Market Database

There's no way around it: This is a lot of work. But the better job you do at the outset, the more this will turn into a mooocho big cash cow. Notice that we're talking about a database here, not just a "mailing list."

Why a database? Look with me at an experience I recently had.

My stepson was about to turn 16, and he would, on a day very close to his birthday, undergo a rite of passage fraught with danger and expense: Getting his driver's license. I had mixed feelings about this, given the amount of time I've spent and gas I've burned carting him here, there and everywhere over the past couple of years. I'm holding on to the belief that his ability to drive himself where he needs to go will be, all told, a good thing.

I bring this up because not long before his birthday we received a letter from our insurer (USAA, which also holds our existing car loan). It congratulated us on the fact that our child was about to reach driving age and suggested various ways in which the company could help us, from finding a new car (either for the stepson or for ourselves, assuming we're passing one of our used cars on to him), to financing the new car, to cobbling together an auto insurance policy for a boy of dubious but rapidly improving driving skills. They even said they have a system whereby they negotiate the price on the new (or new used) car for us.

Needless to say, this timely mailing caught my eye, and I ended up using our lender-insurer for many of the services offered. Which is precisely my point here.

There are few things more valuable to you than a detailed database filled with the names, addresses, and other information about clients who have enjoyed working with you.

Past clients—a poor term since it implies you no longer have anything to do with them—and prospective clients are candidates for Creative Database Treatment. This is a fair amount of work, as I've already suggested, but bear with me. It's more than worth it!

In whatever way makes the most sense to you, gather a bunch of data about these clients and potential clients and keep it in a personally-constructed database. It's a great idea, for example, to hold on to key dates, like client birthdays and anniversaries, and send out appropriate greeting cards.

More to the point, it's a good idea to know client ages and the ages of their children (when they will be graduating from high school, for example—a time when there is a wide variety of possible ways you can provide assistance, from financing for college to an investment house close to the college). You should know what your clients' and their children's major interests are, so that you can help steer them in directions they'll appreciate. Suggested concerts for music-loving clients, sports events, vacation destinations, good restaurants. And you should have some ideas about what they want to accomplish financially and how real estate can play a part through the years.

Notice this change in the assumptions we should now have about the way we do business. We are no longer just salespeople who get their clients through a purchase or sale transaction and then say, "Sayonara." We are advisors who can offer them assistance through each stage of their lives. And if we know when each stage comes along for each client—when a child is likely to be moving out, when retirement is probably approaching—and have it in our database, we know when to send the appropriate letter or make the right phone call.

There are many great database programs on the market, including real estate-related address books and follow-up programs. Find one you like and use it to the maximum.

Step Two: Whom Do You Put In Your Database?

Who are the people in your target market? It may be the residents of a particular community (or "farm area"). It may be the members of a church or club or other organization. It may be an identifiable group, like the shoppers at a food co-op. You may even partner with a few very prominent restaurants or local retailers with great reputations for service and mail your newsletter to their clientele, along with yours. And it could be various combinations of the above.

The point is that your target market should contain a group of people with whom you have some important things in common—a love of living in a certain place, a deep involvement in a church or social or sports organization, a passion for music, or whatever it may be.

The central people in your target market, of course, will be those whom you know well. And you should include dear friends and relatives who live far away–all part of your *sphere of influence*. They are likely to be enthusiastic about your marketing materials, perhaps passing them on—or, at the least, mentioning your name favorably—to someone else who could be moving to your area or could use your services in some way.

The next concentric circle in your target market will be people with whom you've developed a good professional relationship, especially those who have had a good experience of working with you. And the outer concentric circle should include your "farm" area or church group or other body of relatively like-minded people. Beyond that, you should always be ready to add the names and addresses of people who request to receive your marketing materials.

Yes, indeed. I just said: people who request to receive your marketing materials. If your materials are good, if they provide valuable information in a fairly entertaining way, people will want to receive them. This is extremely important, and we'll talk about it further in a moment.

How do you get the names and addresses? If you're using a "farm" area as all or part of your target market, a title company will usually be able to supply you with fairly up-to-date address lists in a particular development. Other than that, you're on your own. Social organizations or church groups tend to have very accurate mailing lists—but they are understandably reluctant to share their lists, so you will need, really, to build your list carefully and gradually, ideally asking each person if he or she would like to receive, say, your monthly newsletter.

The benefit here should be obvious. Seth Godin calls this "Permission Marketing." If you gain permission to send someone your monthly newsletter, he or she is far more likely to pay attention to what you send than if it just arrives unannounced in the mailbox. In no way are you intruding on their time if you send them your marketing materials. Instead, you are gradually building a meaningful relationship with your prospective clients.

As you can imagine, your database is a goldmine that will grow a great deal over time and will need constant expansion and updating. When you find out the name and age of a potential client's child, for example, write it down and get it into your database. Further, make sure there is a way you can call up certain groupings of people, like all the people in the outer concentric circle (general "farm" area or church group or whatever it may be), when you want to send something only to that group.

The True Gold in Your Database

There's a wonderful moment in one of the classic episodes of *Fawlty Towers* when, Basil, the quirky owner of a small hotel, comments on the departure of a rare customer who expressed satisfaction with his stay. "Well," Basil declares to his wife and partner in the business, "a satisfied customer. We should have him bronzed!"

As it happens, satisfied clients are, without any doubt, the most important people in your database. This runs contrary to the thinking of most real estate professionals—who all but forget past transactions and the people they involved, wanting to get on to the next one—but you should court past clients more actively than anyone else in your target market.

They are the ones who will tell friends, family and associates how much they enjoyed working with you. They are the ones who will suggest that people in their social circles ask for copies of your newsletter or pay attention to your newspaper columns. They are the ones who will send people to you who need a bit of advice about a real-estate-related question. They are walking billboards for your services.

One word of caution, though. Many real estate trainers suggest that you constantly ask your past clients for referrals—as if they were holding back referrals, waiting to be reminded to send people to you. I have to say that this can be very annoying and can backfire on you.

Consider: If you see a movie that you like, do you not delight in telling friends about it? If you find a great place to shop, a wonderful new restaurant, a reliable car repair shop—doesn't it give you great pleasure to pass the word around? The best businesses have built themselves upon precisely this principle. People love to share what they have been happy about.

As a result, what I suggest is that, rather than asking for referrals each time you contact a past client, the emphasis should simply be on contacting past clients in ways they appreciate—like sending them informative newsletters. This reminds them of why they enjoyed working with you, keeps the relationship alive, and stimulates precisely what you hope for...referrals of potential clients with whom you'll probably get along very well and productively.

Step Three: Hire A Helper

One of the best things you can do early on, if you can afford it, is to hire someone who will help put together your database and then keep it up to date and will also mail out your monthly newsletter or other marketing pieces. This is ideal part-time work for a young mother or stay-at-home father or a neighborhood teenager you can rely on. It can be done whenever your assistant has the time, rather than on a militant schedule, and it is, for the most part, rather repetitious work that can be interrupted by children or the need to answer the phone. But it's work that becomes potentially more and more engaging, and more and more fulfilling, over time.

You may want to take the initial steps in the creation of your database yourself, both so that you yourself know how it works and so that you know it gets a good start. Further, you may not want to be spending much money on such help yet. But let go of these tasks as quickly and effectively as you can. They are not where you should be investing your time and energy in the future.

While it is a great thing for you to be the one who constructs and fills your database, just as it's a great thing for you to be the one who keeps your mailing list up to date, you'll find yourself moving rather rapidly toward difficult questions about where it's wisest and most profitable to invest your own time. Generally, this question is best answered as follows: Any activity that will serve your present and future clients should take priority—if you have some way of getting the odd jobs in your marketing program taken care of by someone else.

Some way—the best way, generally—is to start grooming your assistant from the word, "Go." This can be a spouse, a reliable child, someone you know who would benefit from having an at-home, part-time job, perhaps (as just mentioned) a young mother or father in your neighborhood. Ideally, though, it will be someone with the personal pride and initiative to develop aspects of the job himself or herself and, crucially, able to stay with the job for many years to come. Indeed, you should build into the job a growing sense of personal responsibility and ownership that includes pay increases as the size of your business and its rewards increase (though not, of course, based on percentages of your commissions).

I hasten to add, if it isn't clear already, that this "assistant" is by no means a full-time employee. You might give certain specific tasks to him or her, like...

▶ Putting labels on newsletters and preparing them for mailing;

▶ Taking the newsletters, appropriately bundled, to the post office for bulk rate mailing;

▶ Developing and maintaining the database of your target market with great care;

▶ Possibly doing some writing and/or editing for you;

▶ And contacting past clients and potential clients, especially those who have won one of your contests.

Your assistant should take ownership of the tasks involved in creating a business-generating database and develop an imagined relationship with all of the people in it, should continually update you on the size and nature of your target market, and should also take on—more and more as his or her experience grows—responsibility for seeing that people in your database receive birthday cards and other special mailings and phone calls from you.

I must advise that the work such an assistant can do for you is invaluable and deserves good pay. Realizing that an entry-level real estate or mortgage professional may not have a lot of money to pay an occasional assistant, I suggest a clear understanding that the potential amount of pay will rise as your success in the business allows you to pay more and his or her tasks increase in size and number. You should create an agreed-upon schedule that maps out when and why income hikes will occur.

You will be working with someone who is rooting for you and is, over time, finding creative ways of helping you serve your clients and target market, and thus helping you build your career. In time, when this works, the assistant becomes a kind of partner to your success.

A Last Few Words About Your Database

You can fill your database with names and addresses fairly easily using rolls provided by a title company and, hopefully, the organization to which you belong and, of course, your own address books. But how do you get the personal information that helps so much if you are to know when a particular potential client's daughter is about to graduate from college? How do you know when to send birthday cards?

There are several approaches to take. First, you can talk to people. If you have a quarterly supplement to your newsletter (which we'll look at in detail soon), you can call on people who have moved to the area and ask if they would allow you to say a few words about them in the newsletter, introducing them to the community. (You can print a few facts about the people, leaving out addresses and phone numbers and saying that, for example, if anyone wants to contact the skateboarder in this new family, they should call you.) If these were your own clients, you may wish to include a photo and a brief testimonial from them. (Keep in mind the power of testimonials and remember to get them! Graciously.)

Second, you can (and, I believe, should) have annual or semi-annual contests that always involve an entry form. Now, the temptation here is to ask for a landslide of unrelated personal information on the entry form, as is often done when you fill in an entry form about a free vacation and later discover that your phone is ringing off the hook with inquiries about when you can come by and pick up your consolation prize at the time-share seller's office.

My suggestion is that you avoid that kind of nonsense. You will receive a dismayingly small number of entries to your contests anyway—at least, at first—and they will be fewer still if people are as leery of giving out a lot of personal information as they should be.

So here's what you can do. Let's say you have an annual Mother's Day contest, in which a son or daughter writes a brief essay about why his or her Mommie deserves to be taken out to dinner at a good local restaurant. Of course, you can ask a few personal questions—like the entrant's age, address, and phone number.

When the time comes and you have a winner for the contest, you will want to turn the awarding of the dinner into a fun occasion. Perhaps you can arrange a meeting of the manager or chef at the restaurant and the child who won the contest. You should have a picture for your quarterly supplement (see below) and perhaps you can get someone from the local newspaper to take a photo as well. (I see a "grip-and-grin" photo with all of you holding the winning entry, smiling deliriously.)

Don't stop there. Make sure you get plenty of information about the child for your article and, if possible, for the newspaper. And get to know the other members of the family. And take notes, especially if you, like me, didn't come equipped with a functional Instant Recall button.

And there's more. The entrants who didn't win should receive small consolation prizes. Perhaps a single rose for their mother (depending, of course, on how many mothers we're talking about here) and/or a certificate declaring them a runner-up winner of the annual essay contest. Either you or your assistant should deliver these—or perhaps you could ask people to come by and pick them up—giving you an opportunity to know these people in your target market a little better. And also giving them an opportunity to know you as a human being, not just a well-dressed real estate professional.

Other contest ideas? Perhaps you want to raise the level of sophistication a bit. Create a survey form, perhaps on the changes taking place in the real estate market or the changes the client would like to see in real estate practice, offering a free dinner for two to the person whose entry is picked in a drawing.

If your target market has a shared interest—be it social service or ridding the community of poverty—then there are clear issues that you would like to address in a survey or in a question-and-answer format.

Annual events provide intriguing contest ideas. As the Academy Awards ceremony approaches, for example, you could create a contest form on which people can note the films, actors and actresses whom they think will win the major awards. At Grammies time, you might ask which artist(s) people think will win the awards for jazz musicians. During major sports events—the World Series, for example—you could ask which team will win and by how many games.

The possibilities are endless. Just make sure that you create contests that are reflective of your own interests and passions, and use them to connect with the people who enter and to get to know them better... and fill your database with all you learn.

CHAPTER TWENTY-ONE

Priming the Pump

X

There are actually two steps to the beginning of a successful marketing program. Unfortunately, most people overlook the first step.

Here it is: You must do what you can to make people aware of you… so that they will recognize, look at, and appreciate your marketing materials (newsletter, newspaper columns, etc.). Until the first task has been accomplished, the impact of the other marketing materials will be somewhat muted. If you just send out newsletters and wait by the phone for the business to roll in, you may decide that your newsletters just aren't working for you—though they probably are… but very gradually.

Time to prime the pump!

Notice that past clients, friends, relatives, business associates, even casual acquaintances don't need to be made aware of who you are. When you send them your marketing materials, they're almost certain to look them over with appreciation every time you send them out.

But people who haven't a clue who you are may very likely toss your first few newsletters into the circular file before paying any attention to them. Advertising experts tell us it takes roughly two dozen "impressions"—experiences of an advertisement—before the average person will even start noticing the ad. Two dozen! We need to short-circuit that statistic.

My colleague Rand was recently talking to one of our long-term newsletter clients who told the story of walking his target market or "farm" nearly twice a month for the first year he was sending out his newsletter. Very quickly, the people in his target market got to know him and became avid readers of his newsletter, and were often eager to discuss it with him when he dropped by. At the end of that year, he had a solid referral business from all the people to whom he continues to send his newsletter. But he's simply too busy now to continue walking his farm, so it takes a while for new residents to start reading his newsletter each month.

This fine real estate professional invested a great deal of shoe leather in getting his career solidly underway. But there are many other ways to accomplish this first step—breaking into the awareness of your target market. We've discussed other ways earlier, in Chapter Twelve. Good news: Most of them can be fun.

For the moment, though, we want to reiterate a few of the most important things you can do.

▶ 1. Gain personal permission from as many of the people to whom you send your materials as possible to keep sending them their way.

▶ 2. Always keep copies of your newsletter with you, or clippings of your weekly newspaper column. Give people a copy if they haven't read it. If it's the newsletter, ask if they'd like to receive it on a regular basis. If they're newspaper columns, tell people where to look for them each week. Very nearly always, you'll have enthusiastic new readers as a result.

▶ 3. Notice that it's important to be able to talk about the content of the newsletter and/or newspaper columns. We call this "Owning Your Marketing Program." Make these marketing materials your very own. Stand behind them. Make sure people benefit from them. Talk about the stories in your newsletters and columns—even to those with whom you already have a relationship. The power of your marketing will mushroom as a result, and you will reach, all the more quickly, the wonderful point where your business flows in consistently, no matter the quality or condition of the market.

CHAPTER TWENTY-TWO
Yes, Newsletters!

)(

I t should be extremely obvious that I'm going to suggest newsletters as the foundation for your marketing program. I've participated in the use of newsletters for the successful development of hundreds of great careers in real estate and real estate finance.

Can we pause here for a few testimonials?

"I've been doing the Newsletter every month since 1988. It is the only marketing I do and it works like clockwork in bringing in clients. We are swamped and a lot of our clients are people who have gotten my newsletter for years and say they only do business with me, even when I tell them they may have to wait." (Buzz Doxey, Sun Coast Financial Group)

"I am very, very busy! Many people who get my newsletter (*Real Estate Report*) tell me how much they love reading it. Also, I have heard from many that they never read the other newsletters they receive but always read mine!" (Ali Burns, Ali Burns & Associate)

"Our newsletters are the only marketing we've done for over twenty years, and we've been extremely successful in this marketplace!" (Bob Bryson, Realatrends)

You can use something else—a weekly article in your local newspaper, for example—but I find that the newsletter satisfies more of the requirements I place on a marketing program than does any other marketing piece.

What Do You Expect From Your Marketing Program?

Nowadays, we see the smiling faces of real estate professionals in what used to be very unexpected places. On the sides and backs of buses. On lighted posters in supermarkets and malls. On bus benches. In shopping carts. On billboards.

Name- and face-recognition advertising is rarely a bad thing. In many areas, for example, it's the primary form of self-promotion that candidates for city councils, judicial positions and other offices use. Yard signs blossom like weeds at election time and, if the candidate is lucky, his or her name will be the one the voter recognizes in the polling booth.

In the case of real estate professionals, name- and face-recognition advertising can prove helpful as part of the initial stage in marketing yourself. (There are less expensive ways to accomplish this, though.) If someone recognizes your name and face, he or she is more likely to pay attention to your other marketing pieces—the ones that convey something of who you are and how you do business and what makes you stand out from the crowd of real estate professionals. We could classify these second-stage materials as "image-building" marketing because they develop an idea of who you are that a future client can relate to and come to admire.

What I want to suggest is that name- and face-recognition advertising is only, at best, the first step in a successful marketing program. When people decide whom to call on for help with their real estate needs, they generally don't make the same kind of decision that they do regarding which city council or municipal judge candidate to vote for. The more positive things they know about you, the more likely it is that you're the one they'll call.

But they don't learn much about you from name- and face-recognition advertising. They see, perhaps, that you have a kind smile. You can afford a good photograph. You may have a catchy slogan. And obviously, you have enough money to mount such an expensive advertising campaign. But they see next to nothing about who you are as a person and professional and why they should feel good about calling you.

Who ya gonna call? Most people, as I've said, call the person with the best reputation—that is, the professional recommended by someone they trust. Ideally, they will have had the kind of experience of you—because of reading your newsletters, or attending your workshops and seminars, or getting to know the you at church or in a social group—that leads them to feel pre-sold on you.

A great deal of name- and face-recognition advertising appeals to real estate professionals because it is rather like having an extraordinarily fancy business card that attracts people's attention and brags that you are a member of the Emerald Jubilee Sales Club (or whatever it may be). But a better use of your money, I would argue, is to send materials to your target market that they will look forward to and enjoy and perhaps even benefit from. Materials that provide a service and say, "This is who I am."

In other words, you want your on-going marketing program to accomplish more than name- and face-recognition among your potential clients. You want it to sell you to them in truly effective ways, so that you're anything but just another pretty face in the real estate crowd.

A newsletter—if it is attractive, well-written, interesting and informative—provides your target market with a sense of who you are, with information they can use and talk about and maybe profit from, and with a deepening sense of already having a professional relationship with you. When someone who has been reading your newsletter for a long time calls, this is not a "cold" lead; it is a warm one. Further, it is very likely someone who will appreciate what you have to offer as a professional, someone with whom it will be very productive and enjoyable to work. And there's even the golly-gee factor when someone actually gets to talk to the person whose newsletter he or she has been reading for several months. You become, in a manageable way, something of a celebrity.

A newsletter does not interrupt and irritate people in your target market—as an unexpected telephone call or knock on the door usually will. It is something that can be read and enjoyed at any time. And it often sits on a kitchen counter, desk or table for several days, especially if the reader found something in it that he or she wants to remember and act upon.

A newsletter, ideally, is like a piece of who you are, out there among your potential clients, continually speaking well of you.

The Many Newsletter Myths And Objections

In spite of a newsletter's proven qualities, many people raise objections and worries about the effectiveness of a newsletter. Over the years, we've heard dozens of them, and here are a few we hear the most frequently.

▶ 1. "But people in my area want something really short. They won't read a four-page newsletter."

Many studies have been done on this and have proven beyond a doubt that a longer piece of writing—if it is well-written, personable and has valuable information—is more effective in mailed advertising and marketing pieces than is a shorter piece. Studies involving vast numbers of mailing pieces found, for example, that there is a 100% greater chance that someone will fully read and respond to a longer letter than to a shorter piece.

A longer letter allows the reader to get to know the newsletter's subject matter at a greater depth, allows a personality to develop in the writing, allows the reader to start identifying with the writer of the newsletter. That's just the way it is; some things will never change. Arguing that people want it short and sweet is like arguing that people would prefer their sitcoms not to have jokes. It's true that you don't want to send out overly lengthy newsletters, but a well-written four-page letter has proven to be ideal.

Have you received promotional letters from investment services? There's an art to writing those pieces, and it always involves staying with the reader for a long time—through a long, discursive letter. By the end of the letter, the reader is often ready to take action.

▶ 2. "But I don't want to bother people every month. I only want to send something once a quarter."

This objection contains two huge and important misunderstandings. First, the marketing materials—whether newsletters or another sort of piece—should never, ever "bother" people. If they do, they're not written well, they're pushy instead of being truly informative and interesting, and they are otherwise offensive in some way. You want to send out materials that are personable, easy to digest, intriguing, informative—letters that treat your readers with maximum respect.

One of the roots of this sorry objection is the belief that advertising must interrupt and bother us—must be what Seth Godin calls "Interruption Marketing." Anyone who has spent any amount of time with a television on late at night can easily come to such a conclusion… but it is terribly wrong. Some marketing pieces are eagerly awaited and happily received. That is how your newsletter should function.

Second, it is crucial to respect the fact that repetition and consistency are key elements to any marketing program. If you are sending out materials only once every three months, you are not impressing yourself into the consciousness of your target market.

Experts say it takes about 24 impressions or so before the average person even begins to notice an advertisement. This is very important to remember as you decide how often you wish to send marketing materials to your clients and potential clients.

We made a significant discovery in our own business regarding this. We noticed that, in all but a very few cases, those who stop using the newsletters we provide have been sending them out on a quarterly basis. And they tend to stop after sending them out three times, on average.

This confirms what my colleagues and I have intuited all along. It just doesn't work to send out a quarterly newsletter – unless (1) it's just a small part of a much larger marketing program or (2) you're only sending it, along with other materials, to a sphere-of-interest mailing list…to people who already know who you are. Even then, though, it makes more sense to touch bases with your target market more often.

Cost, though, is always one of the main considerations of people as they decide how often to send out newsletters. That's understandable, but I readily advise people to send out a much smaller quantity of letters much more consistently than to do a large mailing once a quarter. It's simply a choice between something that works, and works well, vs. something that doesn't work nearly as well.

Needless to say, I vote for what works.

The same can be said of sending three hundred newsletters to one portion of your target market one month, and then three hundred to another portion the next. This works about as well as taking your high blood pressure medication every other day to make it last longer. (And yes, my analogy here does date me, doesn't it?)

▶ **3. "I've been sending a newsletter out for two months now and I haven't gotten a single phone call from anyone, much less a listing or a sale."**

As I've said numerous times already, marketing yourself—as opposed to advertising a house for sale—and marketing to build your career are very different from the usual Direct-Response Marketing techniques used by real estate professionals. And the effectiveness of service-oriented marketing techniques, like sending a monthly newsletter to your target market, should not be judged the same way you judge the effectiveness of a classified ad or other Direct-Response approach.

The fact is, you should never stop using Direct-Response approaches—until your service-oriented marketing builds a strong and consistent referral base. Even then, it's great to use classified ads and similar approaches.

There is another factor. When most people begin a marketing program, they find themselves expecting responses after the first thing they do. Send out a newsletter and...where are the telephone calls and emails? Start up a newspaper column and...where are the fan letters? Why isn't a line forming at my desk, made up of people who want me to list their home or sell them another?

One of the reasons life doesn't work this way has already been mentioned more than once. Studies show that it takes a great many "impressions"—that is, people have to see several ads or columns or newsletters—before people really become aware of you and your message.

Another reason is even more obvious if we stop thinking about our own needs and concentrate on the needs and habits of buyers and sellers. I cited these statistics at the beginning of the book. "Sellers take an average of 9.3 months from the time they begin actively thinking about a sale until the close date," according to an extensive recent survey and study conducted by Hebert Research for House Values, Inc. But once they decide to sell, they "take only one day to select a real estate practitioner." And the length of time from first thinking about the purchase of a home to actually completing the deal is, on the average, 16.7 months—and the buyers "select their real estate practitioner within just one to three days."

Now, this doesn't mean that buyers and sellers make a snap decision when choosing their real estate professional. Quite the opposite! Ever buy a car? Have you noticed that, once you decide what kind of car you want, you start seeing them everywhere? ("Where did all these

Subarus come from all of a sudden, dear?") Similarly, when people are revving up to buy or sell real estate, they are generally spending a lot of time looking at the Internet and at any real estate materials that come their way. At this point, they should be seeing YOU everywhere.

Your marketing program should be aimed at winning over clients who will take perhaps six months or more to choose you. During that crucial time period, you want somehow to be providing them materials that catch their eye, provide valued information, give them an idea of who you are, and gain their trust.

You'll most likely want to use a combination of your own helpful website and newsletters or newspaper articles. And you will want your newsletter or articles to make people aware of your website, and vice versa. Your future clients, more and more, are doing a great deal of research (about buying and selling, about current market conditions, about what they can afford, about the best financing programs, etc.) before they get around to choosing the person who will provide them professional assistance. Ideally, you will want to be building a relationship with them through your marketing program while they're in the research phase of the transaction.

The Hebert Research study concludes, "Consumers choose to work with practitioners for three main reasons: paperwork and legal work; negotiations; and access to listings. And both buyers and sellers tend to select a practitioner based on experience, honesty, and past relationships." Through newsletters, articles, workshops and your website, you can demonstrate these qualities and abilities. "Build it and they will come"…but not as a result of just one newsletter or article. They're taking their time, so stay with them all the way until they decide that you're the one!

▶ 4. "I don't have the time or ability to put out a newsletter each month."

Once the business starts to roll in, you probably won't have time to be rolling out a monthly newsletter and getting it into the mail. As with the database, it may be good for you to develop the first few letters—but here are your options.

• **First,** if you're good at it and enjoy the task and can do it quickly, by all means write and format the newsletter yourself. Then hand the formatted copy over to a part-time assistant who will get it printed and mailed or hand-distributed for you.

There is no more effective newsletter than one that is researched and written by the real estate or mortgage professional whose name and photo are on the front page (and, I hope, on the back page as well). You can write about things that are truly and specifically important to the people in your target market, you can give them a very genuine sense of who you are, and you can respond to the questions and needs of your marketplace. Those who receive such a newsletter feel truly in touch with the sender and develop great professional relationships with you.

• **Second,** though, if you can't create the monthly newsletter yourself, perhaps you can find a part-time assistant who can do so. You can give him or her story ideas, make sure the right things are covered in each letter, and leave the writing and formatting to your ghost writer. And again, the printing and mailing should be handled by a part-time assistant, perhaps the same one who is doing the writing, perhaps not.

• **Third,** you can find a newsletter service that will provide newsletters in quantity, with your name and photo prominent in the newsletter's format, with the feeling that you could have created the newsletter yourself, with copy that is relevant and that you can relate to in a positive way. Additionally, the newsletter should allow you to add a bit of your own localized copy, perhaps on the back page (generally the first thing seen by those who receive the letter). Your letters should be prepared for mailing and taken to the post office by your part-time assistant— but ALWAYS READ THE NEWSLETTER YOURSELF CAREFULLY BEFORE SENDING IT. You not only want to guard against any errors in the newsletter—but, even more important, you also want to make sure you have studied what you are sending into your target market so that you can discuss your newsletter's contents with interested clients and potential clients.

Those are the options. Let's explore some of the details in the composition of the newsletter.

CHAPTER TWENTY-THREE

Your Newsletter: Get It Right, And Get It Read

W hat is the right kind of content for a newsletter? Good place to start. (We'll talk about appearance and formatting questions in a moment.)

In often subtle ways, your readers will come to associate the nature of your newsletter's contents with who you are. Your newsletter, after all, builds an idea in readers' minds of the person who sends it out. It is an "image-builder."

This raises a few important questions. How do you want people to see you? What qualities do you want people to associate with you?

Most likely, you want people to see you as a very knowledgeable professional whom they can rely on for helpful assistance, someone who knows the business, someone who approaches life in ways they can relate to. Maybe even someone with a sense of humor they appreciate.

With that in mind, it should be obvious that any factual information you can provide about the real estate market, the direction interest rates are taking, recent tax legislation and other real-estate-related legislation, along with tips on how to engineer the best sale of your home, how to save money on the purchase of a home, and how to invest successfully in real estate—all of this is both intriguing and helpful to most readers.

Still, many people in this business are at a total loss regarding what they should put in their newsletters. "What do people want?" they ask. In reality, they should be asking, "What can I share about the things that fascinate me the most in my business?"—rather like Joe Coulombe (of Trader Joe's) filling his stores with the products he loves the most. Find the answers to that question—what fascinates me the most?—and you will be sending out material that is at once very interesting and very clear in its depiction of who you are.

What You Might Not Want To Include

For some reason, PR people who dabble in creating newsletters for real estate and mortgage pros can't resist including something like a "Recipe of the Month." Before you do so, ask yourself: Do I want people to associate me with cooking? If you relax after a long day and evening of work by expanding your gourmet cooking abilities, you may indeed want to write a little article about that each month in your newsletter and include recipes you've developed. If not, however, stay away from including a recipe. Same goes for a Craft-of-the-Month, etc., etc.

If it's something you're not particularly interested in, it's filler. Avoid it.

If it isn't something you yourself are interested in—or, ideally, feel passionate about—don't include it in your newsletter.

You may want to include a bit of comic relief, though. But approach this with care. What's funny for one reader may be outrageous, offensive, or allergy-inducing for another. We'll discuss this at more length in just a moment. For now, though, let's think of good humor breaks in your newsletter.

Books of quotations are often a great source of humor. There are also sections of the newspaper that detail weird but true stories. And there are books detailing everything from the funny garblings of English to be found when traveling in foreign countries to unexpected facts about our nation's presidents (including the president who went skinny dipping in the Potomac and was trapped by a newspaper reporter who refused to move out of sight until the President gave her an interview). I am talking about fairly intelligent humor here that doesn't depend on putting people down, doesn't generalize about human beings, lifts us up rather than bringing us down.

Being Respectful Of People's Hot Buttons

Even seemingly innocent material in your newsletter can prove surprisingly offensive to some readers. Examples from our own experience:

• After attending a wonderful seminar at a California Association of Realtors® convention, and then reading a book by the seminar leader, on using the principles of feng shui in preparing a home for sale, I wrote a newsletter article that briefly summed up some of the better points. A client called up and said he couldn't use the newsletter because, from his own religious perspective, feng shui is an oriental mystical system that he doesn't want to be associated with.

• In a July newsletter, I closed an article with the words, "Happy Birthday, America." A client called and said that, according to his religious training, it is wrong to celebrate birthdays. He therefore felt he couldn't use the newsletter.

These examples show how very careful and thoughtful you must be in order to avoid treading on anyone's toes. (You can probably imagine how we sweat bullets over the holiday greetings we include on the December newsletters. You will very likely want to take the same kind of care with your words.)

There is, however, another side to this story.

What if, for example, your primary target market is made up of the members of your church community? You are unlikely to want to hold back on or dilute your own belief system just because you don't want to offend the stray atheist on your mailing list. Indeed, it is precisely because your belief system is a good match for your potential clients that you are marketing yourself to your church congregation. You want to work where your passion lives, where your deepest sense of what is right motivates all you do. And you want people to know that.

It is a similar situation for the successful real estate professional I've mentioned who markets herself to the environmentally-aware people in the local population. Obviously, she makes very clear who she is and what she stands for in all of her marketing pieces, sending copies of articles and flyers about local services and groups that are working for a more sustainable future. She doesn't worry about offending potential clients because anyone who is offended by her materials would most likely be a poor match for her, resulting in a strained professional relationship.

Perhaps the most remarkable example of a specialized target market I've ever seen came across my desk when a client mailed me a marketing piece sent to her by a friend of a friend of a friend. The real estate professional in question was marketing to members of "naturist" organizations (read: nudists). I mean, why not? It's fun, in any case, to imagine the listing appointments.

And there is something else—a truth that is illustrated by the experience I had with telling my clients about my wife's death… in a newsletter that reached thousands of readers. Giving away genuine parts of yourself—your interests, your sense of humor, even your passions—can help develop a relationship with your potential clients, making them feel they know and trust you. This is extremely important. After all, the more like-minded your clients are, the better your transactions will be. The better your transactions are, the more quickly your client clan grows—and the less likely you are to face the poison of an angry client spreading negatives about you.

One last point, and this too is very important. The reality is that if you are not offending someone, you're probably not saying much of any value, and people aren't reading the spineless, soulless mush you send out anyway.

This is a tough one. You don't want to offend people. You want to honor diversity, different customs, and different religions. But you don't want to avoid important subjects just because they make some people uncomfortable. Example:

A brand new real estate agent, getting her first shipment of newsletters from our company, called in an awkward state of distress. "You talked about the budget deficit and national debt in the newsletter," she wailed.

"Yes?" I said, perplexed.

"Well, my manager agrees with me that I shouldn't talk about those things in my newsletter because they're political and they might offend someone."

If the real estate market turns to a great extent on the direction interest rates are heading, and if interest rates may spike upward because the nation's budget deficit appears to world investors to be utterly out of control, you bet you should make some mention of that in your newsletter. You certainly don't need to take a partisan approach; budget deficits are an equal-opportunity, bipartisan problem. Leaving the fact that deficits are escalating and world confidence in the dollar is plummeting out of your newsletter under these circumstances is like pretending there isn't a dead elephant in the living room. And the readers of your newsletter will realize that they can't count on you for thorough, incisive, honest discussions of real-estate-related subjects.

I suggested to my new client, by the way, that if she wasn't able to send out a newsletter that discussed the possible effects of our budget deficits, she really should find another source of marketing newsletters. It's a point I will always stand by: If you are uncomfortable with the materials you are being sold by your marketing company, find another company.

The main person to avoid offending with your newsletter is yourself, after all. Which is another way of saying that you really do need to feel at home with the marketing materials you send out; they really do need to represent who you are.

Three Examples of Newsletter Stories

Two of these stories went into newsletters sent to specific target markets in California; the third went out nationally. The first two are sensitive to local problems and needs. All of them convey important information that could conceivably save people a tremendous amount of money.

Objection: Some real estate professionals might worry that they seem to be positioning themselves as tax and insurance experts with these stories. This is not the case. All such stories either state explicitly or imply that the next step is to talk to a licensed tax advisor or insurance professional. The crucial role of you, the real estate professional here, is to be the one who helps clients and prospective clients become aware of important concerns and opportunities and helps put together the best questions to ask of their tax advisor or insurance advisor (the people licensed to give the appropriate advice, since most of us aren't licensed to practice law or to give tax advice or even to sell insurance).

Another objection: Yeah, but I'm still not a tax advisor or an insurance advisor. Why can't I advertise what I do? Why can't I have stories about real estate practice?

You can and must. But in this case—and here is why I included these stories first here and saved for last the story on the importance of pricing a home well within the current verifiable market range—is that you are positioning yourself as the "point person"…the all-around source of good information who puts all your energies into serving all of your clients' needs, increasing their profits and security and decreasing their costs and hassles in everything related to their home.

When it comes to the home and real estate investments, therefore, YOU are the person to talk to first!

Here are the stories, therefore. They were all distributed in the second half of 2005.

[First story]
Making Tax Savings A Certainty

As you doubtless know, the tax code allows us to exempt up to $500,000 in home sale gains from our personal residence if we're married and filing jointly, $250,000 if we're single. Here in California, this liberal tax benefit is no longer adequate to cover the gains from a home sale in many cases. In a future issue, we'll look at a strategy of tax deferral for the sale of very highly-appreciated homes, but in this issue, we'll look at several of the fine points regarding the $250,000/$500,000 exclusion.

First, let's review the requirements to qualify for the exclusion. First, you can only use this exclusion once every two years. Second, you must have lived in the home in question a cumulative total of 24 months in the five years prior to the sale. Third, you must have owned the home for at least 24 months.

There are exceptions to the second rule. Let's say you only lived in the home for 12 of the required 24 months. If you had to move for what the tax code terms "unforeseen circumstances," the home will qualify for one-half of the $250,000 or $500,000 exclusions. (If you had lived in the home for six months, the home would qualify for one-fourth. Simply divide how long you lived in the home by 24.)

What is a qualifying "unforeseen circumstance"? The IRS has a specific list that includes natural disasters, a change in employment or self-employment, divorce or legal separation, or multiple births from the same pregnancy. Talk with you tax advisor to see if you qualify—

and note that there are rather broad potential understandings of many of these circumstances, notably "change in employment."

Okay. There are also exceptions to the third rule. You must own the home for 24 months unless you took title to the home through an exchange of like-kind investment properties, in which case you must own the home for a full five years before it will qualify for the gains exclusion. This would occur if you exchanged properties and received, perhaps among other properties, a rental home that you later convert to a personal residence.

This may sound ridiculous, but we have to be very clear about what we mean by "live in the home." You must occupy the home as your primary personal residence. If, for example, you own more than one home, you must be able to prove that the home in question has been your primary residence. The IRS has several tests, including whether you received your bills at that home, whether it was the location of the church you attend, whether it was your address for voting purposes, for banking purposes and so forth. (More reason to consult with your tax advisor!)

A few other points need to be made about the requirement that you live in the home—and these may surprise many taxpayers. First, you have to live in the home a cumulative 24 months over the five years prior to the sale, but that doesn't mean you have to live in the home a sequential 24 months, nor do you have to be living in it at or close to the time of sale. Indeed, you don't even have to own the home the same 24 months that you live in it. It is possible, for example, that you rented the home, starting five years ago, lived in it for a year and bought it, then moved out for two years, renting it out to others, then moved back in for the final year.

Other fine print matters? What happens when you have a home office within your personal residence and you've been depreciating the space and deducting expenses? Do you have to separate that out from the $250,000/$500,000 exclusion? Thanks to a fairly recent IRS ruling, the home office is included in the exclusion. You need only recapture depreciation (at a 25% tax rate). Notice that this is not the case if your home office is in a structure that is separate from your residence.

And what happens if you own a parcel of land that is attached to the property on which your home is located? It can be included in the gains exclusion. Not only that, but you don't have to sell both the residential property and the parcel to the same person or at the same time—though you do face a time limit.

As you can see, the opportunities for tax savings are remarkably liberal. Since the $250,000/$500,000 gains exclusion went into effect, the IRS has issued a stream of clarifications that, in general, favor the taxpayer. But one thing the IRS will not do is to bend the rules or the timing requirements.

Therefore, it's crucial that you keep good records of dates of purchase and occupancy, have the assistance of your tax advisor, and call on your real estate professional for help as well. There is a great deal of money to be saved here. Do it right!

[Second Story]
A Few Facts About Earthquake Insurance

Fact #1: It's expensive. Indeed, it is expensive enough that only about 13% of homeowners carry it.

Fact #2: It's become more affordable. Insurers in our state carry "mini policies," thanks to legislation after the 1994 Northridge quake. You can buy insurance, for example, with a hefty ten or fifteen percent deductible.

Now, that's a lot of deductible if your house is worth a few million dollars—or even if it's worth far less. But, as insurance experts note, the deductible is obviously vastly higher if you don't carry any quake insurance at all.

Fact #3: It may make financial sense for you today. Let's say your coverage would cost about $800 a year. Over the thirty year life of your mortgage, that adds up to a hefty $24,000. However, the policy could easily pay $2,400,000 to many policy holders in case of a devastating quake—a ten-to-one bet, in other words.

Fact #4: The destructive results of a quake could prove even more arduous today than they were a decade ago. Why? First, because house prices have risen so dramatically that homeowners have that much more equity to protect. Second, because recent changes to the bankruptcy rules make it far more difficult to simply walk away from financial obligations. "Remember," warns Nancy Kincaid (a director at the California Earthquake Authority), "you will still be responsible for your debts, including mortgage and home-equity loans, even if your home is destroyed."

Fact #5: There are several things you can do to protect your home from damage. "If you have a home with soft-story construction or a raised or partially-raised foundation," you can have the foundation bolted and brace the cripple walls. Further, you can use special safety straps to brace your water heater, large or top-heavy furniture, and electronic equipment, and use museum putty to hold china and collectibles in place. (And you can obtain rebates of 50% for these products at various local home-improvement stores through November.)

The Anza desert, Yucaipa and offshore Crescent City all experienced quakes recently. Now, while there is little demand for insurance or quake-protection products, it's a great time to be the one who protects his and her home and lifestyle. With all of the above potential benefits—including the least expensive insurance we've ever seen—the unavoidable fact is that it's worth looking into earthquake preparedness.

[Third Story]
Getting The Most For Your Home

In any real estate market, the appropriate price to ask for your home is best found by reviewing all recent sales of homes that are comparable to yours. You will want to know the details both of the house's condition and of the sale itself. One house may have a pool. One sale may involve a good deal of seller financing. All such factors are important to the sale and need to be factored into your understanding of what the current market value of your home is.

This has been covered in other articles in this series but deserves to be repeated: Homes priced within a range justified by the current market sell faster and generally for more money than homes that are priced higher than that market range. This may at first seem counter-intuitive, but—especially in an age when home buyers are doing their own sophisticated analyses of market values—an over-priced home makes no more sense to a potential buyer than an overpriced carton of

Cheerios. And buyers are very unlikely to pay any attention to a home whose price makes little sense.

Now, there are still sellers who are persuaded—in spite of what the actual market data indicate—that a particular real estate agent can "get" a higher price for a home than other real estate agents can…as if real estate professionals fooled or strong-armed their clients into offering foolishly high prices for homes. It doesn't work that way. The truth is, one real estate professional may have a far more effective marketing program than another, bringing in more potential buyers and giving your home the benefit of favorable advertising and presentation, and thus bringing in the best possible price and fastest and easiest sale… but that all starts with an asking price that is reasonable and accurate in today's market.

Formatting And Other Important Details

A newsletter is not something you wish to create with a felt-tipped pen (unless you're a remarkable artist). The rule that has always made sense to me is that you want a newsletter that looks very professional but also looks like you did it yourself. You don't have to look far to see questionable newsletter formats. When PR firms are handed the task of making a newsletter, they tend to make it look like a PR firm designed it, of all things, and then had it printed in colors and fonts that shout at you. There is no sense anywhere in the letter of the presence of the person whose photo actually appears on the newsletter. (Indeed, the photo is usually black-and-white, while the rest of the newsletter is full of blazing color and often full of color photographs of models acting like happy clients.) In short, it looks like the real estate professional was slapped on to the front and back of the newsletter as an afterthought.

You want, instead, to look like the writer and designer of your own newsletter, even if you plan to tell people who receive the letter that you didn't actually write it. You hired someone else to—someone who would create what you would create if you weren't so busy with your business.

I suggest, therefore, that the top of the first page be made up of what could be called your masthead. It should include your newsletter's name, your photo, your logo, your slogan, your company name, address, phone numbers and any email, fax, and cell numbers you wish to include. This should be tasteful, and it should be precisely the same in every issue. (Okay, if you go on an exercise spree and lose twenty pounds, you can certainly take a new photo if you want.)

About that photo: It wants to be crisp, professional, but also friendly. I believe I've seen every eccentric approach possible. Woman with dog. Man in prayer. Many men holding phones to their ears and smiling. Woman standing by 'For Sale' sign attaching a 'Sold' sign. Etc.

By and large, my advice is to let the photo just be about your face, your smile, what you look like. Wear a nice piece of clothing for the shoot. Leave the dog at home...unless your target market is some canine protection association. (Gee, wonder what the photo for the naturist real estate agent looks like. Oops, sorry if that thought offended someone.)

This photo, as I've mentioned before, should be as central to your marketing as a logo or slogan. It should look like you, therefore, and look decently business-like. Not a 20-year-old senior prom photo. Not a soft focus glamour photo. Just a good, representative photo of you, the way you really look, with a genuine smile on your face. Taken by a real photographer, not your brother-in-law in the garage with a disposable camera.

I suggest that your stories, which start below the masthead, be presented in two columns with headlines. Ideally, neither story will end on the front page; both will say, "Continued on page two" (or on page three). This small detail helps assure that people will get to the inside of your newsletter. It's also a good idea to have a box on the front page that mentions what's inside this particular newsletter. (INSIDE: "Market taking off again!")

It is good to intersperse your copy with subheadings and, if possible, clip art. (You can buy disks full of clip art at a relatively small cost.) The art serves to break things up, so that the reader's eyes don't see a wall of print and start skipping through paragraphs. Take care and use professional clip art, not cartoons that appear silly or juvenile. It's also good to include the occasional boxed section—"Notable Quotables," for example, a monthly group of humorous and/or touching quotations from famous people.

The back page, unless you send out your newsletter in an envelope (which you should avoid to save expense, and to make sure people don't throw out the envelope without even glancing at your newsletter) will probably include your mailing surface, where you'll put the address label, next to another photo of you, and another naming of your company, along with its address, the relevant phone numbers, etc. This generally leaves half the page for your own copy and, as mentioned before, since this is probably the first thing people will see when they pull the newsletter out of the mail, you should mention the most area-specific or target-market-relevant news in this space. It's a good place for local news, for a discussion of the local market, for photos of recent clients with their brief testimonials, etc., and perhaps for another box that includes another headline for a story inside the newsletter.

The size? We produce one newsletter that is a letter-sized piece of paper folded in half. It stands out rather nicely in the mail. And we produce several newsletters that are 11 inches by 17 inches, folded in half, and then once again. All, therefore, are four-page letters—though the fourth page is somewhat dominated by the mailing surface.

Mailing? Go to your local post office and find out exactly the way your local official wants your newsletters folded and addressed and stamped. I know this will amaze you, but I have had experiences of several postal service officials who seemed intent on dissuading me from bothering them with a newsletter…especially one I wanted to send out bulk rate. You need to smile and soldier through the apparent obstacles and, hopefully, walk out with a workable relationship with your postal official. It's also possible that an official in one post office branch will have a significantly different interpretation of bulk mail rules than an official in another branch. Be certain you know exactly what your post office official needs and wants. And when your assistant takes the monthly mailing to this person, he or she might want to take a small gift, smile a lot and act very sympathetic regarding the postal official's insufferable problems. Sigh a lot. (No, I'm not putting down all postal workers—not by a long shot. But I seem to have met a few who were obviously and blatantly in the wrong line of work.)

One last simple question: **Can I just write a good letter on my own letterhead each month?** The answer is a definite yes. It may not carry the weight that a newsletter does, it may take people longer to get around to reading it, but it also may be a far better representation of the real you. And that is one of the main points of the exercise.

As I mention more than once in these pages, people generally like to know a bit about the real estate professional they feel inclined to call upon for assistance. They like to build up something of a relationship with you, following some of the major events in your life (like that trip to Europe, that hike to the top of Mt. Whitney, the birth of your child, the graduation of your child) and becoming increasingly aware of the things that matter to you, the things that make you laugh, the things that light up your emotional dashboard.

A letter, obviously, can convey all of these things. It can be an occasional checking-in, a kind of on-going personal and professional journal (perhaps a more formal version of what can be accomplished with a blog on the Internet). The important thing is to keep the letters consistent—in tone, in quality of information, in when the letter goes out each month.

Keep it happening and the letter will surely keep your business happening. But if there are reasons that you don't feel you can produce the letter and send it out regularly, align yourself with a newsletter service that works well for you.

CHAPTER TWENTY-FOUR

The Quarterly Supplement

G ood news! The Quarterly Supplement is entirely optional. But do consider it.

What I suggest is a simple letter, typed by yourself on your computer and either inserted in your regular newsletter or mailed separately once each quarter. This doesn't have to be terribly sophisticated in appearance. In fact, if it has a hot-off-the-press look, all the better.

The primary contents of this letter should be news about the local market. This is a great place to list recent sales prices, announce local upcoming events, and include any other pertinent information. You can also announce contests and even include the entry forms as a part of your supplement...and announce the winners in it as well. And you can include information about people in your target market, especially people who are just moving into the area. Use the power of testimonials here, remembering always to treat your clients and potential clients with great respect—and to honor any desire for privacy they may have. The point is to include them in a fun and celebratory way, not just to paste them into your supplement as if they were a paid advertisement.

Further, if your target market is, say, made up largely of jazz lovers, you can write in your supplement about jazz, about recent performances and new recordings, perhaps about the jazz festival that is coming up. If your target market is devoted to environmental issues, you can inform them of the work of relevant organizations in the area and other related news, as does my successful friend. If your target market is essentially a "farm," a residential development, then any news regarding the neighborhood and, if it has one, the homeowner's association may be appropriate. If you are marketing to naturists— well, hey, I haven't the slightest idea what you should cover, if you'll pardon a ridiculous pun.

Why go to the trouble to create a quarterly supplement if you already have a space in your monthly newsletter that is filled with your own localized copy? Largely because the newsletter space is fairly limited, and it would be difficult to get an adequately detailed list of comparable home prices into it. Further, the quarterly supplement looks like something you wrote and added at the last moment, having filled it with up-to-date data and area-specific information. And you want your newsletter to have a very consistent quality that readers can rely on, whereas your supplement allows you to break format, include news you just wouldn't put in your newsletter, and get special attention for other information you may want to share with your target market.

If you are using a newsletter service, you will find the quarterly supplement a bit labor-intensive. But your occasional assistant can do a good deal of the work, letting you devote more of your time to what serves your clients the most. But you will have more clients to serve, I am certain, if you go to the trouble of doing a quarterly supplement.

A great alternative: You can develop a monthly email service that includes the target-market-specific information you would put into your Quarterly Supplement. It has the benefits of being extremely inexpensive and very timely. The big issue, though, is making sure you have the permission from each of your recipients to send it to them. It's work, but it's productive work, enlarging relationships with potential clients to include such permission.

Read on!

CHAPTER TWENTY-FIVE

What About Email?

A lthough studies have shown that at least 70% of those with email services have bought at least one item that was advertised via email, most of us are convinced that email has failed as an advertising or marketing device. And with good reason(s).

First, most of us have experienced the huge and bothersome numbers of pointless and aggravating emails that clog our email box all too frequently. Much to the consternation of the Hormel Meat Company, we call this stuff spam, and we've become so annoyed by it that filtering programs have been developed.

The problem with most of these filters is that they throw out the proverbial baby with the bathwater. Emails coming to you from addresses you haven't authorized your filtration system to accept often get lost, and they could have proven valuable to you. Likewise, any marketing email program you may launch will face this filtration problem. We'll look at a solution in a moment.

Second, in any case, is the fact that there are so many quirky geeks on the loose who find curious pleasure in spreading obscure, destructive viruses. Many people, usually wisely, have moved to a policy of not opening attached files on emails unless they are certain of the intentions of the person who sent the email.

Third, most of us have received countless email offers to be ripped off. "Hi, I'm a voodoo Yoruba priest from West Africa who wishes to transfer a billion dollars into America. Honest! Please send me your bank account information and, while you're about it, your social security number, so that I can transfer half of my funds to your bank account, with the agreement that you will then transfer 75% of those funds to my new American bank account, keeping 25% for yourself as a fee."

Such offers would be impotent and laughable if the gullibility and generous nature of many of us didn't lead us to take a chance on such bogus offers. The results, in any case, have shown up in hundreds of thousands of cases of identity theft. Even those of us who haven't been caught up in such scams feel as if our fingers have been burned, and we are extremely unlikely to respond to most offers that arrive by email.

Sounds like we should just avoid marketing by email, right? Wrong.

Here are the steps you should take. First, and most important, get the permission of everyone on your emailing list to send them your materials.

How do you do this? As always, think of the client, not of your needs to market yourself and increase your business. You might think, for example, that you should avoid sending your materials to a client more often than once a month. Change your thinking! How often would you like to receive a useful, illuminating insight into the condition and direction of the real estate market and of interest rates? Phrasing it that way changes everything. Now we're talking about a service that many people will very gladly grant you permission to provide them.

Would the people in the midst of your target market be interested in a monthly email that details the sales and condition of the market specifically in their neighborhood? The answer in most cases is a resounding yes.

How, then, can you provide a service that people will appreciate via email? That is the question…and the answer could create a wonderful, efficient, inexpensive portion of your overall marketing program.

What does permission look and sound like? You can send a letter or a postcard, ideally something that offers a preview of the service you will be providing, and say that you or your assistant will be calling soon to get their permission to send the email to them on a regular basis. You'll also, of course, be collecting email addresses in the process.

A second idea concerning your email program, then, is to make sure not to send your email as an attached file. Your material should be in the basic body of the email so that any worries about opening a corrupt or virus-inflicting file are minimized.

And the solution to the problem of not being able to penetrate people's email filters? Again, it's a question of permission. When people give you permission to send them an on-going email, you can remind them to set up their filter to accept your email.

When is the best time to start such a program? One idea is to send out the letter or postcard regarding the email program a week or so after sending out your first or second regular monthly newsletter. Thus, when you call to get permission to send emails, you are reinforcing the newsletter—perhaps talking about it during the call—and you also have the credibility you've gained by sending a professional, high-quality newsletter before talking about sending a professional, high-quality email. Immediately, you develop a certain amount of synergism with the two marketing pieces.

And so long as they truly provide service to your recipients, they will work. The whole marketing program will exceed the strength of the sum of its parts.

Further, there are other uses for emailing programs—ranging from an early-warning system with which to alert your target market of contests you are initiating, news with extraordinary local relevance, and personal matters involving residents in your target market. For example, you could make a habit of mentioning the names of people who were cited in the newspaper for their achievements, charitable work, or simply for their age.

You could, as I suggested in the last chapter, create a more frequently-assembled version of the Quarterly Supplement, discussed earlier. You could also use your email service as a way of keeping your name in front of your peers in related businesses (see Chapter 30). The possibilities are endless.

CHAPTER TWENTY-SIX

The Internet: Work In Progress

The Internet is currently (as this is being written) one of the Next Big Things. Ironically, it wasn't that long ago that it was the Great Menace, destined to eliminate all real estate professionals from the face of the earth.

What happened? Unfortunately, too few people know very clearly what happened. Rumors and exaggerations abound. So let's see if we can clear this up a bit.

When the Internet began to gain wide acceptance, there were remarkable misunderstandings of what this new communication device could and would do for us. People began to fantasize a brave new world in which potential homeowners simply clicked online from the comfort of their home office, scanned a bunch of available properties, decided on one, and filled in an online offer. The loan would then be handled online, as could matters of title and all the other details in a real estate transaction. After an hour or two—bada-bing bada-boom!—another new homeowner. And who needs a real estate professional or mortgage professional when you can just point and click? Think of the money to be saved! Now think of all the reasons people won't ever want to buy a home this way.

Why? The reasons are many—I mean, who's going to buy a car without taking the opportunity to kick the tires, take it for a test drive, do some research about it and ask a bunch of pertinent questions—but let's cut to the chase and look at what may be the most important of them all.

Few of the Internet's early True Believers stopped to consider the fact that the Internet doesn't SELL. It stores and provides information, and it takes orders. That's it. Those two features it can master incredibly well. Indeed, we have only scratched the surface in discovering all that the Internet can do for us. But it cannot and will not sell us a house.

This started to become evident when people noticed that a growing percentage of American buyers were initiating their research for the purchase of a home—and, possibly, sale of an existing home—by reading through the ballooning amounts of relevant information on the Internet. Through Internet sites, potential homeowners were finding out much of what they needed to know about the areas where they were considering buying; they were studying the kinds of mortgage programs they would choose from; they were figuring out how large of a loan they could probably afford, and thus the price range in which they would be looking; they were learning the steps they would take to find and purchase their new home.

Okay, this means they were learning that they didn't need a professional real estate advisor, right? WRONG! The more people have learned about real estate transactions, the more they have realized how much a good real estate professional is worth to them, and how best to get all they want from their real estate agent. They can, after all, ask the right questions. They know what they're talking about.

Those who have done their preliminary research on the Internet, studies have universally shown, are actually far more likely to call on a real estate professional for help with their home search, their negotiations, their paperwork, the details of the closing. The more you know, the more you know what you can get from real estate professionals.

This means real estate professionals very nearly have no choice but to become experts in all they do—because the majority of today's clients have much higher standards and expectations than people generally did a decade or more ago, when they were working with the legendary Joe Doakes, Realtor®, who knew how to make a terrifying cup of coffee, how to drive people to houses, and how to scribble a few standard phrases on a short purchase contract, and very little more.

Viable Uses Of The Internet

Now that our profession no longer believes the Internet is going to eat up the jobs of all agents and intermediaries, the pendulum has swung in the other direction, and we now have True Believers who are certain that the Internet is the only marketing program you need. Just get yourself a great website and buyers and sellers will soon be swarming all over it, begging you to represent them in their deals.

That the Internet can become an important—indeed, a necessary—part of your marketing program is true. That it can become the be-all and end-all of your program is nonsense.

It is a very different medium from classified ads in newspapers, from newsletters, from someone knocking on your door and asking if you or someone you know is thinking of buying or selling a piece of real estate. Again, the Internet is not a good substitute for a human salesperson and advisor, though it offers mountains of information on most subjects. It is also not an advertiser in the usual sense, as we'll see in a moment. Instead, it is a storehouse of information and advice for your clients—past, present, and future—and should be approached as a way you provide service, even giving away "free samples" galore.

Early on, most real estate firms decided the Internet must be a great place to advertise listings. Compelled by the kinds of habits they developed when writing classified ads for newspapers, they carefully withheld key information so that people looking at a listing would pick up the phone to ask for the missing information.

It didn't work and is even less effective today. Most people will not be manipulated into picking up the phone for missing information in a website. This is very important. I'll say it one last time: **The Internet is, above all, a source of vast amounts of information**. People click their way to and from different websites, seeking the information they want and need. If you withhold that information, they're gone in an instant, clicking their way to another site that will give them the information they need.

And they leave with a bad impression of your site. You don't make friends, and certainly don't convince people to keep coming back to your site, by trying to get them excited about something, then withholding key information—like price, availability, location, etc.

The other side of this coin, though, sparkles rather brightly. The Internet is the place where you can give people ALL available information. Unlike a classified ad in a newspaper, the Internet doesn't charge you by word or by line. You can tell your whole story, make your entire promise, recite your mission statement, show photographs of and discuss the features of every one of your listings, even offer virtual tours of homes.

Further, you can provide a loan calculator; you can give background information on the area in which you work; you can offer links to other valuable sources of information on local schools, parks, cultural life, and other amenities.

Your website, rather than being the advertising device that gets people interested in you and the services you provide, becomes the place people can go, once they're interested, to find more information.

This means something else got them interested in the first place and motivated them to seek out your website. This is a simple problem that many who believe the Internet will solve all their marketing problems overlook. You must create strategies for driving people to your website.

Why Would Someone Look At Your Website?

There are a great many reasons:

▶ 1. **Because they were driven there by a search engine**—a Google, a Yahoo, or something similar. This means someone typed, say, your city and the words "real estate" into their browser, and yours was one of the sites that came up. There are definite tricks that can help increase the number of people arriving at your site, and an Internet pro should be able to help you with them. (More on that in a moment.)

▶ 2. **Because they saw your URL** (your address on the website) in your newsletter or in another of your marketing pieces. Which brings up a crucial point: Your website should be woven into your overall marketing program, and every printed marketing piece you put out into the world should have your site's address prominently displayed on it, often with reasons that might inspire the reader to check the website out.

▶ 3. **Because you are running an advertisement whose sole purpose is to motivate interested people to look up your website.**

The Internet Solution to an Advertising Puzzle

We publish prospecting materials, as you doubtless know by now. We've always stumbled around the issue of marketing our newsletters and other programs effectively. There are several dicey problems.

First, most people aren't tremendously familiar with this form of marketing. It's important to explain this pretty thoroughly so they can decide on whether they want to look more deeply at using newsletters and similar materials.

Second, most advertisements only get a cursory glance. You need to be able to show off the benefits of using your services in a few seconds. There's simply no way to do this in a newspaper or magazine ad. Further, such advertising is rarely cost effective, and the alternative, mailed pieces are similarly restrictive—because they involve huge mailings, not just regular mailings to a well-defined target market.

So the issue here is finding a way to tell our story, on the one hand, but realizing that there aren't cost-effective ways of doing that in an advertisement.

The solution? (Yes, Virginia, there is a solution.)

We started running very small ads in industry publications—boxed display ads back among the classifieds and smallest advertisements. Our little ad features a photo of one of our clients, usually someone who is reasonably well known in the industry, along with a two- or three-line testimonial. The only other copy says, "See for yourself! www.rightsidemarketing.com 800-456-4395."

That's it. You get the message in a second, and your curiosity is piqued enough that you are likely to check out our website, where we tell you our whole story, give you our promise, and show you our entire line of products, including sample newsletters and price lists. Indeed, you can download order forms and fax them to us.

And it works, largely because all of the information is there. The website becomes the guy who sits there answering questions, filtering out people who really aren't interested, and bringing aboard people who are.

The website, therefore, takes over a lot of the explaining that you would otherwise be doing. It isn't the ad; it's where people go to respond to the ad.

Internet Etiquette

There are many things about the strange cyber-universe that should be understood and respected. As I've mentioned, for example, people are inclined to move quickly from one part of a site to another; and this should be made as easy as possible for them, or they'll move, possibly with even greater ease, to someone else's site.

The web, therefore, implicitly allows its users a sense of power—the power of the click—and most people don't like their power to be messed with. A web site that demands information, requires you to fill out this form or that and give up the safety of your relative anonymity—this tends to ruffle people's feathers. "User-friendly" is an obvious rule; "honor the user's identity (or anonymity)" should be another.

Above all, it's crucial to realize that people will fly like manic sparrows through most websites and from one to another. That's just the way it is. Therefore, even though you have the opportunity to tell it all in your website, you also have to catch the attention of each person who visits the site. You have to grab them (in a friendly fashion) by the eyes and hold on to them, showing them how easily they can get to precisely the information that interests them.

It is important, unless you have a fair amount of expertise as regards building websites and making them effective, to call on professional help in engineering your own website, therefore. Get someone who can help make your site attractive, give it a bit of visual pizzazz, and organize all the material so it's easy for the user to get from here to there. Increasingly, though, there are also site-building services on the internet that allow you to use templates to build an effective and attractive site of your own.

We have only begun to make use of the special features that a website may allow—from music to mind-boggling graphics to charts to stunning photos. Realize, though, that your website doesn't have to win awards. It simply needs to give its visitors a good idea of who you are, what you do, how you do it—the "promise" of the "experience" they'll have of you (as was described earlier in this book).

Do You Have To Have A Website?

Today's True Believers are constantly saying that you have to put up your own website or the market will pass you by. (Remember that the True Believers were saying a few years ago that real estate professionals have to find new lines of work because the Internet is about to make them obsolete. Who, in fact, was made obsolete here?)

No, you don't have to have your own website. But I believe that there are enough things you can do with a website today to make it truly cost-effective in most cases…and more effective uses of your website will evolve in the near future. It's doubtless worth climbing aboard today.

But keep it in proper perspective. Your website won't become your sole marketing program, won't drive all your business to you, won't fix you a good cup of coffee in the morning. It has limitations, like any single portion of your overall marketing program.

The bottom line is to assemble a marketing program all of whose ingredients you can afford and keep running regularly and continuously.

One Last Thought About The Internet

Unlike, say, a personal newsletter that goes out to your carefully-constructed target market, your website is easily available to anyone with a computer…anywhere in the world. This is exciting, yes, but it isn't entirely efficient. You really can't market your services to the whole world. You can market yourself as the woman to call when someone wants to find in house in Tuscaloosa if you live there, but it's something of a hit-and-miss affair. You can't market yourself as the listing agent to the world. Nor can you market yourself as the real estate professional to call, whether you live in Nairobi or in San Diego.

Notice that the Internet seems to serve us best as a combination super-business-card/brochure and FAQ answerer. It tells our story to those who have been made interested by an ad like the one described above, by something in a newsletter, by a referral, or something similar.

One of the big complaints we have heard about the Internet lead-generating systems goes something like this: "Don't give us any more of those Internet prospects. The conversion rate is too low." And it is, indeed, difficult to deal with someone whose actual interest is completely indefinable until you talk with him or her—someone who, interested by something in a website, happened to call you.

These aren't people who know who you are (unless they've picked up a feeling for you from your website). And there's something important we can extrapolate from this: The Internet is unlikely to be the foundation of your career-building marketing program. It is far more likely to be the library that stands behind all you say, the resource that people can visit for important information, the mega-brochure explaining what you're up to and the listings you have to offer.

As such, it can prove to be a fabulous ingredient in your marketing gumbo—but not the only spice in the bowl.

Have We Only Tapped the Surface?

The short answer is a definite "YES!" We have only scratched the top of the iceberg here; there are tons of uses of the Internet waiting below the surface of our awareness for us to find and make use of.

One simple example:

The Blog.

Essentially a bulletin board that offers multiple opportunities to jump around to other sites (through hyperlinks), a blog's core purpose, thus far, has been to allow a small group or an individual to share information and ideas with readers. It could be, but rarely is, an evolving newsletter with bits of timely information about real estate. More likely, it's a giant miscellany sharing the multiple interests and fascinating finds—from movie reviews to videos of old Beatles hits to political opinion to how-to advice—that one person is kind enough to share.

What does this have to do with marketing yourself as a real estate professional? You'd be surprised.

For one thing, there are increasingly huge numbers of people who surf the Web, and they return to sites that offer fascinating tidbits and don't try to sell them something.

Running a blog allows you to share who you are in many ways because you are sharing your interests, values and all that matters to you.

This brings up old worries. What if I lose a deal because someone finds out I'm not an Episcopalean zen Buddhist? What if I offend someone by praising a film they dislike? What if I lose the business of people who hate bloggers?

The issue here, though, is to let go of those imprisoning fears and let your actual self—professional, caring, playful, creative—out into the world so that people who can relate to you will turn to you for help with real estate matters…precisely because they are presold on you.

As blogger Ardell DellaLoggia, an associate broker in a Kirkland, Washington office, says: "Blogging is how you advertise who you are so you get the clients that are most compatible for you." Ardell writes about experiences she has in her real estate work, questions raised by clients, issues that arise in the course of showing properties and marketing listings. Readers often identify with the questions and come to trust the human being giving the answers. [Assuming she is still at it, you can check out Ardell's blogs at *searchingseattleblog.com* and, with other writers, at *raincityguide.com*. For an example of a wide-open approach to blogging, check *growabrain.typepad.com/growabrain/real_estate/index.html*. Check also the blog run by the former real estate editor of the *New York Post*, now a real estate professional and investor in New York City, Ali Rogers: *frontporchllc.com*. Arranged primarily in a question and answer format, it is immensely readable and enthusiastically personal. Of course, be sure to check out my blog at: *youarenotahouse.blogspot.com*.]

Amazingly, Ms. DellaLoggia started attracting clients with her blog only a few weeks after getting it online. And she found that the clients she attracted were people who were ready to buy a home and were ready to trust her and work efficiently with her. They seemed already to know her.

This is a very far cry from the often-repeated complaint about more anonymous Internet-sourced "leads," who are extremely difficult to work with precisely because they know nothing of you and aren't willing to treat you with trust.

Obviously, if everyone in real estate has his or her own blog, the effectiveness of this way of sharing information for marketing purposes will diminish. But that is no more likely to happen than universal use of newsletters, which have been around for a long time (I've been writing them, as I've said repeatedly, for over twenty-five years), and have certainly never come near to saturating the marketplace.

If you are so inclined, you will very likely find it extremely profitable to pioneer new uses of the Internet, basing your work on the principles we've talked about in this book.

CHAPTER TWENTY-SEVEN
Newspaper Columns

Okay, it's time to move on to other marketing programs, some of which, admittedly, we'll pay only brief attention to, sort of the way I pay attention to the cricket scores on BBC radio. I'm just not that interested, and often because of my own experience of the program.

We'll start, though, with newspaper columns, which I'm quite interested in. I've been writing them for nearly twenty years.

This is, I fear, a mildly frustrating subject, though. Why? Because it's such a good idea and, thanks to the expense of placing what is, in the newspaper's eyes, an advertisement in the paper every week, it's also a rather expensive idea.

It's a good idea—no, make that a great idea—because it allows you to have not only your name and face out there constantly where people can see them and remember them; it also allows you to provide a valuable service for free, and people will associate your expertise and your commitment to service with your name and face. And being in a newspaper greatly enhances your credibility . What more could you ask from a marketing program?

Well, you could ask it to be a bit more affordable, for starters.

At the same time, it's important to notice that you may find yourself slightly ambivalent about suddenly having a target market that includes the entire city where you live (and, most likely, adjacent little cities as well). This may sound great because it's very broad coverage, and indeed, it's wonderful, though potentially a bit cumbersome. But it isn't quite as likely to feel like a personal service as will, say, a newsletter you seem to have written and gone to the trouble to mail specifically to them each month. As a result, the effects of an informative, small weekly column every week in the local newspaper may be rather slow to develop.

But they do develop over time, and generally in a big way! As people become more and more aware that you are the person who has been

Malibu Real Estate Review by Chris Cortazzo

THE LILTING LANGUAGE OF TITLE TROUBLES

Have you ever noticed the aristocratic-sounding way attorneys speak of the title to a property being questioned? For one, just the fact that a question has been raised through legal channels puts a "cloud" on the title. That means we're no longer 100% positive that the property is truly yours and yours alone.

If there is indeed a cloud—if, for example, your second cousin twice-removed believes he has a right to partial ownership—a legal action is taken to decide who is right...or to "quiet the title," as if it had suddenly developed a case of the screaming meemies.

Now, if this happens to you, you'll be extremely glad if you made sure that the title was recorded in your name as soon as the property became, so far as anyone then knew, yours. And you will be doubly or trebly glad that you hold a policy of title insurance on the property because it will almost certainly be up to your title company to quiet title and make it 100% yours again. They have lawyers who know how to do that, and they pay them accordingly.

Take full, recorded title to any property you purchase or receive as a gift or in any transaction, and always insure your title to make certain you don't have to pay further to prove in the future that you are the owner. For assistance call me at 310-589-2472 or visit my web site @ http://chriscortazzo.cbso-cal.com.

Chris Cortazzo is a Realtor with Coldwell Banker Previews in Malibu.

providing the good, useful information every week, they tend to think of you the moment they hear the magic words, "real estate." And that, friends, is a wonder greatly to be desired!

A weekly newspaper column should...

- Have the same format and the same photograph each week, all presented in a very professional way;

- Contain a very brief article (of about 150 to 250 words) regarding a specific topic, written in a clear and entertaining way (though there isn't much space to be clever or funny);

- Always endeavor to associate you with the local community and marketplace;

- Appear in something other than the real estate section (because more people will see and read it in other sections of the newspaper; the real estate section, after all, is where you place your classified ads, not your "institutional" ads); and

- Make it very clear how to contact you.

CHAPTER TWENTY-EIGHT

Postcards?

X

"I don't know what you do to get your leads," I heard a powerful real estate broker say not long ago to a huge audience of real estate professionals. "Maybe you send out postcards or something."

There is no way to say this delicately. Even very intelligent and powerful real estate brokers, after many years of managing vast chains of real estate offices, don't know any more about marketing today than they did when real estate was but a gleam in their youthful eyes. "Postcards or something"?

Whenever I shifted a new piece of my marketing program into gear in my early years in real estate—and I was always thinking "career," not just "next meal ticket"—it would bring this response from my company's management. "Gosh, Bill. Sounds like a good idea. Tell us how many listings and sales you get from that."

I remember these people with great affection, but also with this sober bit of wisdom: Do NOT put much stock into any of their marketing advice."

Remember, marketing isn't solely a matter of making the phone ring and having to deal with people who really don't want to talk with you…having to wade through a swamp of skepticism about who you are and what you know and whether you are the slightest bit trustworthy. Ideally, your marketing clears most of that away, and people call you because they already like you.

That said, we turn to postcards. A lot of people in real estate seem to love postcards—at least, briefly. In theory, the idea of something that doesn't cost as much as a newsletter, doesn't require much effort to create, and can be glanced at quickly by the person who receives it… it all sounds great, no?

No.

You may as well simply send out your business card once a month.

Even a highly imaginative postcard—why, even a card that has a photograph on it that people like so much they put it on their refrigerator door—tells your potential client next to nothing about who you are, why they should call on you, why your name should be synonymous with great real estate practice in their minds, why they should recommend you to friends.

A few summary judgments: Don't even consider a postcard program that isn't visually superior. You want, at the least, to be associated with good taste as a result of sending out your postcards.

Do consider postcards that offer up the kind of little real estate column that you might use in a newspaper. But don't expect it to be saved, much less savored. Don't expect much productive exposure from it. A weekly newspaper column is generally a far better bet, even if the type is no larger than what you can fit on a postcard if you are saying anything of substance.

If your target market has a "theme"—if it is a church or social group, or a list of people who love a certain restaurant, or everyone who ever attended the local folk festivals, etc.—then you might support the rest of your marketing program by sending out, perhaps on a bimonthly basis, a specially-developed line of postcards that your target market will appreciate and enjoy. Scriptural quotations that mean a great deal to you would be good for a church group, for example. Or photos of folk artists for that folk music group (with your own photo on the mailing side of the postcard). Etc.

Further, there are careful uses of postcards or notes that can bring immense rewards. For example, people will always look with interest at a postcard that shows them a local home that is for sale and describes the home, including the asking price. Similarly, they will often look with interest at a postcard that tells them the home sold, though their interest is frustrated if you don't name the selling price. Send these postcards out to people who live relatively near every one of your listings—or, what the heck, people far and near—and you will generate the impression that you're the one to call in this area. After all, everyone seems to be listing with you. And you seem to be getting the homes sold.

Postcard or note in an envelope? I vote for a postcard, because you don't need someone to open an envelope to get at your message.

Yes, there are reasonably good uses that can be made of postcards, as you can see. But postcards are NOT a worthy substitute for newsletters, which remain the most effective possible representation of who you are. Newsletters will be read, saved, clipped. Postcards, even if they sit behind magnets on someone's ice box, will gradually be taken for granted like that nice painting of Aunt Mimi in the powder room, and your postcard program will lose more and more of its effectiveness. Think of postcards, therefore, as potentially productive add-ons for a comprehensive marketing program, especially when used as announcements of open houses and recent listings and/or sales.

But use your newsletter to stay in fuller communication with your clients, giving them a deepening sense of who you are.

CHAPTER TWENTY-NINE
Plenty Of Weird Stuff

One of the enjoyable things about going to a Realtors® Association convention is meandering through the mammoth rooms that contain the booths with the marketing materials, new technology and various other curiosities, and people anxious to sign you up for this or that.

Now, over here, folks, we have the Carnivorous Plant of the Month Program. Your clients and potential clients will receive, every month, a creepy-looking plant that is not only fun to look at but also reduces the bug population in the household. The kids will be thrilled as they watch the Venus Fly Trap polish off your common housefly. Etc.

And here, folks, we have great little gifts for clients that you can print your name and phone number on. Take, for example, this fly swatter (wow—there's a theme developing here!) that you can order in designer colors and even with a hole in the center of the pad, so that swatting flies becomes something of a sport.

Okay. I admit I made these up. Or maybe I elaborated a little bit on things I've actually encountered. But they aren't that far from the real things.

Gimmicks. And answers to empty dreams.

Because marketing has remained such a mystery to the real estate profession, wherein we are still looking for that magic pill, those few words we can memorize, that new technology, whatever it may be, something that will bring in new clients instantly, with a mere snap of the fingers, leading with astonishing rapidity to multiple commission checks. Riches galore, like the winnings on a television quiz show.

But that's an old and outdated, faulty vision of the real estate profession, and I'm certain the reader of this book is quite aware that you can't trick people into becoming your lifelong clients, referring friends, family members and associates to you because you know the thirteen magic words to close a deal or have precisely the script for every sales occasion.

Still, there is and probably always will be a steady outpouring of marketing programs du jour—sort of like new diets appearing every month in the magazines that line the supermarket checkout aisles—trying to lure you with the siren call of the "new way," the "instant client ionizer," the "five sentences for success," the "portable charm doll," the "power closing formula."

No—bottom line, it will always be YOU, exactly who you are, giving the best that you have to give, and attracting people who will want to work with you, who will trust you, and who will very enthusiastically help you create and increase the size and quality of your business.

CHAPTER THIRTY
Marketing To Your Peers

I've mentioned that it took me a while—about six months—to build the foundation for a steady stream of clients. When it rained, though, it poured.

One of my favorite memories, very clearly etched into my gray matter, involves the time I created my first "peer flyer" with brief descriptions of the thirteen listings I had in my target market. I went from real estate office to real estate office, leaving my flyer on the salespeople's desks.

In the office of someone who had been working the same target market ("farm"), a fellow looked up when I cheerfully laid my flyer in front of him.

"Hey!" he called out. "What's this?"

"A few listings I'd like your help in selling," I responded, and it was the flat-out truth.

"Few?" he said. "Few?" He counted them. "Thirteen is a few?"

I just smiled and moved on—because, along with wanting his help in selling my listings, I also wanted to impress on him that I was now the owner (so to speak) of this target market. And that, too, is the flat-out truth.

This wasn't just a macho need to show the older real estate professionals that the new kid in town had a plenty big Trabuco (an odd kind of gun, in case your imagination was veering in another direction), though it didn't damage my ego at all to hear people suck in their breath as they counted the number of listings on the flyer. Fine and good, but the real point was something that has evaded most people in the business.

It pays to market yourself and your work to others in the business. Or, as we saw earlier,

Service-Oriented Marketing Principle #8: Do Not Limit Your Friendships To Your Own Office Or Company, And Do Not Let The Misleading Idea That Someone Is Your "Competition" Keep You From Creating Beneficial Relationships With Such People.

The people who are usually considered "the competition" in this business are actually your assistants in getting listings sold. If you keep them informed with valuable information, you'll find them calling when they have questions about the homes in your target market or the problems in your area of expertise. When they have clients who are looking for a home like the ones you typically list for sale, they'll call you to see what you have available.

I would only add one word of caution. Back when a hot market and a burgeoning set of cable television channels had resulted briefly in real estate-oriented television channels, I signed up to do five-minute news broadcasts in which I sat behind a desk, looking like your garden variety talking head, and read the latest real estate-related news in my best announcer voice. It was fun, but it wasn't profitable.

I decided to stop when I, as listing agent, received an offer from a pro I'd always hoped to work with, a very nice guy who worked a different part of the county than I did. After we'd helped put together a transaction that suited both the buyers and the sellers, he and I ended up standing by our cars, talking for about an hour. He admitted that, having seen me on television, he'd become afraid of working on a transaction with me, worrying that I might prove "too knowledgeable," might show him up somehow and create an unfair advantage for my clients.

Enough with the television program, I decided. That wasn't the result I'd hoped for at all.

Moral of the story? Keep your intended audience in mind—their needs, their wishes, what they want to accomplish—in all your marketing efforts. The TV show was a bit of an ego duster; it wasn't really that much of a service to anyone, and it left a slightly sour taste in the memories of my colleagues in the business.

Are There Other Kinds Of Peers?

Yes, indeed, and they can steer a great many superb clients your way. Bankers, lenders, financial advisors, stock brokers, and others who provide financial advice and help to their clients love to have people they can trust to help their clients when the need arises.

How do you build a relationship with such professionals? There is nothing better than meeting with them, talking, finding common ground, developing a professional friendship. Even if you have the opportunity to do that, though, you will still want to stand out in that person's memory, so that you're the first person who comes to mind when he or she wants to send a client to someone who will provide superb assistance with real estate matters.

Therefore, you can add such people to your newsletter mailing list. And you can develop a weekly email that follows economic indicators—something that may prove both intriguing and helpful to people in the financial advisory businesses.

There's also a side benefit, as I've found in my long-term experience of writing a weekly financial update: It forces you to stay on top of the credit markets and the direction of the economy from a real estate point of view. This is helpful in a great many ways, not the least of which is that you can always speak knowledgeably with clients about where interest rates may be headed and why, and what they can reasonably expect the real estate market to do over the coming few months.

And another benefit: You build an extended team of people whom you, too, will call upon to help your clients with specific financial matters. There is a possible synergism here that will add great value to what you offer as a real estate professional.

But the bottom line is this: Getting very positive referrals from peers in related professions brings in more "warm" clients, and your business continues to mushroom.

CHAPTER THIRTY-ONE

Putting It All Together
In Your Own Marketing Program

Ta da! You now have the basic ingredients out of which you can build your own successful personal marketing gumbo. Granted, other ingredients exist—and there are many that may come to mind as you combine and streamline the ingredients presented here—but it is time now to get it all together and get started!

Let's look at a couple of likely approaches. How your marketing program will look depends on a large number of factors, ranging from how long you've been in the business to how much you can spend on your marketing to what the needs and interests of your target market may be.

1 – New to the Business

Unlike people who dive into real estate careers in their home towns, I did two things at once: (1) I went into real estate and (2) I moved to southern Orange County. I therefore had no family or friends to enroll as my first real estate clients. Indeed, I had no one at all.

I had, in fact, a wonderful little Volkswagen beetle, a terrible car for showing properties to people. I had a couple of decent suits and perhaps six ties, a few white shirts and plenty of underwear. And, but for the "Fast Start" training I took, sealed in a learning chamber with other neophytes at a major real estate company's chief Orange County location, I had virtually no idea of what I needed to do to move in the direction of a steady income in this business.

The first thing you learn in real estate, after all, is that you can wait for something to happen, but it will be a long, long wait. You have to make it happen yourself. As a teacher I admire said, "If you want your ships to come in, you have to send them out first yourself."

I was completely dependent on my marketing—and, as we will discuss, on such activities as holding open houses and answering the phones in the office—to create any business, and it quickly became clear that some kind of marketing program would be crucial.

I picked a neighborhood target market (a "farm") and began to make myself visible. I'd been taught to knock on all the doors in my farm area in "Fast Start" training—to start up conversations and drop in the "close": "By the way, are you or is anyone you know thinking of selling or buying a home?" I wasn't all that keen on this approach, even if my company had supplied one microwave oven—for the entire county—to be awarded to someone who filled in one of the cards I carried around while knocking on all the farm's doors.

What worked, instead, was to use the door-knocking as an excuse to get to know my market area as well as I possible could—its history, how the development was built, who lived there now, what the needs of the community were. I attended homeowner's association meetings, listened long and carefully. I sat in the living rooms of long-term residents. I talked, but mainly listened, to many people.

That was, I must insist, an integral part of my marketing program. Here are the other things I did.

I sent out a monthly newsletter that I wrote myself. It talked about the real estate market, which was just yawning, stretching and coming to life at the time; about the national economy; about any little bits of real estate-related news I could find; and about news of the local community.

I also sent out, every month, a sheet that gave prices for recent sales of neighborhood homes. I didn't give out the addresses, just the model numbers, a code everyone understood. Since home prices were starting to climb relatively quickly, everyone was extremely interested in the likely market value of their own home.

I also created a number of community events, ranging from a local haunted house for Halloween to a neighborhood Arts & Crafts Fair where the locals sold crafts and art they had created over the course of the year (an event we put on every Thanksgiving weekend because that's a great time to buy seasonal gifts) to a summer games festival, with races and swimming and a baseball game, a weekend's worth of events, lots of prizes and praise.

Lots of work? Yes. After a time, I wasn't running the Arts & Crafts

Festival or the Halloween house, but they continued on for several years. As my time was taken up with the work I was doing for clients, my marketing became, above all, a pair of monthly mailings.

Now, knowing what we do about marketing at this point, the following should be obvious. The three most important aspects of this marketing program were:

▶ 1. That the newsletter and comp sheet were interesting and informative, and that they always looked pretty much the same, so that people began to recognize them immediately and to associate them with me. The key here, along with user-friendliness, is consistency—using the same photo of yourself, the same format, the same ink and paper colors, the same quality of information.

▶ 2. The other aspect of consistency—one that not only helps people remember (and appreciate) you but also gives them the impression that you are reasonably well organized and can take care of their business efficiently—is getting your newsletter out every month, preferably at roughly the same time of the month.

▶ 3. Lastly, the newsletter (and, to a degree, the comparable sales flyer) always gave a sense of who I am, what I like, what makes me tick… and a good deal of intriguing and helpful information. It was (and is) always honest, never saying it's a hot market when it's not, never trying to portray real estate transactions as anything other than what they are—that is, never down-playing that they involve huge decisions, very careful negotiations, and an awareness of myriad legal/tax/financial matters—but always seeking to expand people's sense of the financial benefits of owning a home. A mix, therefore, of the personal (asserted rather gently) and business and economic news. No recipes. No crafts of the week. Only subjects I wanted my clients and prospective clients to associate with me. (I love good restaurants, bodysurfing, reading, running, hiking, living lightly on the earth and other delights—and I was always willing to put in a few words on those subjects.)

Okay. That's one marketing program. Two mailed pieces a month. You could limit that to one piece. You could even mail one piece every other month, though that is far less effective. A quarterly mailing is—well, repeat after me: How many times do you have to see an advertisement on television before it begins to make its way into your consciousness? 24. Right! Keep that in mind. A quarterly mailing just isn't enough. Repetition is a blood brother of consistency in a good marketing program.

Obviously, you don't have to use a newsletter as the flagship of your marketing program. I have a good friend who sends out a packet of real estate-related information every two months. The program is consistent enough that he has trained me to recognize each mailing immediately as one of his. And because he's kept these mailings coming to me for a year now—and no one else is mailing us anything other than an occasional postcard promoting a listing they've taken locally—his marketing has begun to stand out.

My preference, though, is a newsletter that can be personalized in some way. Something that will just keep going, even when you are so busy with your clients that you don't have time to add any personal material to the newsletter.

One last issue: This isn't cheap. The postage alone is very costly. (You should generally send your letter out by bulk mail to minimize that cost.) But it's as important to your career—assuming you want a career instead of an experience of wondering every month or two if you'll ever have another commission check—as exercise is to the health of your body.

Start small, if necessary. Send out a few hundred newsletters. Work up an understanding with a local restaurant or other merchants and leave your newsletter there for customers to pick up. Put a little promo for the restaurant or other shops in the portion of your newsletter that you can customize, and work up occasional mutual promotions. Example: If it's possible to set up a small area where musicians can perform in the restaurant, you may want to hold auditions for local high school small jazz groups and folk groups, then have the winners play limited engagements in the restaurant.

Notice what I just did. I suggested you start small, stay within your budget, then my mind went racing all over the town for ways to maximize what you are doing while spending the least amount of money to expand your marketing efforts. Notice, too, that it looks like a lot of fun!

Over time, your mailing list will grow. We have clients who send out more than two thousand newsletters each month—and, as they report, they in turn have clients who expect those newsletters to arrive at about the same time every month...and wonder where they are if they're late.

2 – Been in the business a while

Let's say you've been sending something out regularly for a number of years, and the response is good, but you'd like to further solidify your market share. You have a wide range of possibilities to consider.

You may want to add the weekly email service that provides peer professionals a real estate-oriented economic update. You might want to send out a biweekly fax to peer professionals—people who are likely to start sending you a steady stream of referrals—that talks very specifically about what is happening in the local real estate market and deals with current prices.

This would be an add-on, supplementing your existing marketing program with another piece that increases the effectiveness of your marketing. You would make an effort to contact and gain the permission of peer professionals to whom you will send the email or fax—"Permission Marketing." You are, after all, building a relationship through these weekly or biweekly pieces, and you will hopefully have further contact with each of the people who receive them.

Though the creation of such pieces is time-consuming (note that there are some companies that create these for you), an emailed or faxed letter is extremely inexpensive. Unless laws change, it costs virtually nothing to email a letter to dozens of peer professionals, and a fax only costs the price of the paper you've printed it on, though the use of faxes is more limited by law to people whose permission you've gained. This can be a great vehicle for constant contact with people with whom you will send clients back and forth.

The other extreme is to take on the entire town with a weekly newspaper column. You will almost always have to pay for it, and it is expensive. It is also something that ideally should be done in conjunction with other pieces, like a newsletter, but it can over time cement your grasp on the local community. Thus, it is ideal for an independent brokerage or a real estate professional seeking to have an extremely strong and recognizable presence in the area served by a local newspaper.

And if you haven't yet done so, you will want to build a presence on the Internet. You will want a website that acts as an in-depth brochure and information source and helps to market listings. You may want to include a blog that acts as a journal of your experiences in real estate and serves to educate your clients and potential clients through the power of story.

You will certainly want to tie all of these elements of your marketing program to one another, so that every printed piece has your website URL on it and your website promotes your newsletter and other marketing pieces. In this fashion, you drive people to your website efficiently, and you create a marketing synergism in which multiple exposures make you all that much more memorable to the people in your target market and beyond.

3 – Too late for a newsletter?

No, it's never too late. You can start up a marketing program at any point in your career. People who start in the business during a real estate boom often feel no need for a marketing program per se until the business slows and they notice that they are small fish in a big bowl which is remarkably crowded with other fish.

That's a good time to rethink your real estate career, and to create a newsletter or sign on to a truly workable newsletter service. Having read through the descriptions of various forms of marketing, you can doubtless choose ingredients that appeal to you and put together a marketing program that you will stay with for the remainder of your career.

Just make sure your marketing program represents you well. You need to feel at home with it. You need to believe that it is portraying you in a reasonably honest and creative way. You need to identify with the level of service it represents. You need to own it.

Don't Try

A real estate professional, just breaking into the business, is trying to build a marketing campaign that will help bring in the business and leave time to do the business right when it does come in. She decides to try a few things and see what works for her.

"Try" is the dangerous operative word there. While it is important to be able to drop something that clearly doesn't work—as Coca Cola once did with its new formula, returning to "Classic Coke"—it is equally important to see that a marketing program is not a trial balloon. It's a long-term strategy that you plan to stick with through your entire career. It helps define you, it helps give your career direction, and those in your target market assume that it—and you—will continue to look the same, just as Americans had grown to assume that Coke will taste the same.

If you are stepping into the real estate business with limited funds, you will want to develop a marketing campaign that expands gradually. Perhaps you will want to send out newsletters to a relatively small group of people each month. You may also want to create an inexpensive "ice-breaker"—a seminar you sponsor, a contest, a civic event, or any other of a number of possibilities—that makes people aware of you and makes them more likely to look closely at your monthly newsletter.

There are three key rules as you create your marketing program in its earliest stages:

• **First,** do not develop something you cannot afford for more than a few months; make sure you start at a level you can afford and build your program as you are able to.

• **Second,** do not try a lot of different approaches. They will eat up your money and pay few if any returns.

• **Third,** think long-term—because that's what marketing is, a long-term program that will build and nourish your career for as many years as you are in the business. Decide on a program that represents the best of who you are and how you intend to do business, and stay with it, letting it grow as your business grows.

And so imagine…

Your monthly newsletter has just arrived from the printer and, as always, you are pleased with the look of it, the feel of it. You sit down in a quiet place and read it through, every word of it, and you feel very good about the information you will be sharing with your clients and potential clients. You write notes in the margin of your reader copy, leading questions you want to ask some of the people who receive the letter—especially those that pertain specifically to the plans they've hinted about.

Your assistant presses the address labels on to the newsletters and, once that's done, you go through the mailing quickly, writing very brief notes on a few of the letters—"Haven't talked with you in a while. How are you?"—and your assistant packages the letters carefully and takes them to the post office.

In a few days, you get a call, the first of several. "Hi, this is Ken Corll. Your newsletter reminded me—I've been meaning to call you and thank you from the bottom of my heart for the jazz trio play-offs you sponsored at Giancarlo's a couple of weeks ago. Wow! What a great afternoon and evening! I would have gone and enjoyed every minute of it even if my son hadn't been playing in one of the groups. Must be a lot of work putting that on every year."

"Yes," you admit. "It is a lot of work. In fact, about a week before each year's show, I swear to myself that this is the last time I'll do it. Then the day of the show arrives and I just settle into the joy of watching kids make music, and by the time it's over, I'm ready to start on the next one right away."

"Guess it's a little like running a marathon," Ken suggests.

"Couldn't say. But it's a lot like arguing my body out of bed to go to the gym on a Saturday morning. I hate the idea all the way to the gym and love it all the way home."

"I can relate," Ken laughs. "You know, I've also wanted to thank you again for the fine newsletter you send me every month—gets here like clockwork. Very thought-provoking stuff. I always get a few ideas that will probably save me some time or hassle or money at some point. In fact, I think you sent me to my accountant on a fact-finding mission that ended up saving me a few thousand bucks a couple of years ago."

"That makes me very happy."

"Me too, believe me!" Ken enthuses. "Anyway, the last reason I called today is a sort of good news/bad news thing. I got a promotion—a big one—that's the good news. But it's going to involve moving to the city where the corporate offices are located. That's the part I'm not entirely enthusiastic about. I need your help. Could you come by one night soon to talk with us about selling our house?"

"Thursday evening soon enough?"

"How about seven-thirty?"

"See you then, Ken."

PART FIVE

Jump-Starting Your Career

CHAPTER THIRTY-TWO
Getting To Those First Transactions

Okay, I'm going to assume you (1) haven't had many (or any) transactions yet or (2) haven't yet gotten past the point where your deals come sporadically and unpredictably. Even if this doesn't describe you, please stay with me here.

How do you generate your first deals? You'll recall that I began my real estate career in an area where I knew virtually no one. (Even if you've been in real estate for years, you can have my experience by moving to a new area and facing the sobering fact that, all of a sudden, no one knows who you are or what you do.)

There are two key points here:

First, fake it until you make it. In other words, get proactive...fast.

Second, use the power of story.

And what, you may wonder, do I mean by "fake it until you make it"? I mean that, even if you have no listings yourself, you'll want to act as if you do. How? It's not very difficult, though it involves tact and energy.

Find someone in the office, a pro you get along with well, whose listings include the sort of homes you plan to build your target marketing efforts around. Perhaps it's the neighborhood. Perhaps it's the amenities. Perhaps it's other matters involving location. (One important factor involving location: Ideally, the home should be well-located for open houses, and thus relatively visible to passing motorists.) Perhaps it's the profile of the owners. Whatever it is, pick a house and build a marketing campaign for that house.

Your marketing campaign should include...

• A descriptive flyer—or even a brochure—that you will develop for the house, something that tells the story of the house (more on this in a few moments).

• An in-house printed guide for those who visit the home, telling them room-by-room about the features of the home, including photographs.

• Open houses…you should hold your pretend listing open three or four days a week, especially weekends, advertising your open houses by sending announcements to everyone else in the neighborhood and in your target market. (On any mailing you do regarding this listing, you will want to name the listing agent and then name yourself as real estate professional and marketing manager.)

Present these ideas to the listing agent. Ask him or her if you can act as "marketing manager" for the listing, explaining your plan. Make the agent aware that none of this will cost him or her anything. It's your way of getting into the business before you have clients of your own. After all, you expect to generate several clients from the open houses you'll hold and, perhaps, from the mailings you do. The benefits to the agent should be reasonably obvious—the clients are going get special attention and the house will be more likely to sell.

When you find an agent in your office who is willing to work with you—and this is where tact becomes important—it's necessary to carefully explain to him or her all you do, reaching agreement before you do anything. You don't want to look like you're trying to steal clients…and, indeed, you're not. You're expanding the marketing of the home, hoping to generate new clients for yourself. (Remember, for example, that open houses generate about 95 buyers for properties other than the open house itself for every 5 buyers who might end up making offers on the open house.)

You will want to go with the listing agent to meet the owners of the house and to tell them what you intend to do. (Hello, you are the lucky winners of a free, innovative marketing program! No—don't say it quite that way. Even though it's the truth.) Tell them what you plan to do, and gather as much information about the house—when they bought it, what improvements they have made, in what special ways they have enjoyed living there, the profile of the buyers for whom the house seems most appropriate—and examine the house very carefully. Either photograph it yourself or have professionals do so. (A good digital camera can turn you into a professional photographer, and several commonly-used computer programs can turn you into an astonishingly good flyer- and brochure-maker.)

Okay, one minor word of warning. You are developing your own listing/marketing style here. You don't want to make the process so time- and work-intensive that you won't be able to get through it when you have more than one listing of your own to work on.

But that's just my point, really. You want to develop a marketing program for your listings that truly sets you apart from other real estate professionals. What might that include?

• The brochure or flyer, which you will mail to an extended list of people—residents of the neighborhood near the listing and people in your target market mailing list to whom you'll want to give actual samples of your marketing program.

• The in-house guide, scrapbook copies of which you'll want to give both the home's sellers and buyers when the deal is done.

• "Open House" announcements—probably postcards (yes, postcards). And you'll want to include special reasons for people to come to the open house, like perhaps a drawing with a prize that leaves you with a pile of names and addresses and related information. Those attending the open house should leave with a copy of the flyer or brochure, of the in-house guide, and of your newsletter. It's a very good idea, too, to include other real estate professionals in these open house invitations, and to have a special day or two when a free prize goes to an agent who leaves his or her card in the "Realtor's Basket" at the open house. And it's even more important that all real estate professionals leave with a copy of the brochure or flyer and the in-house guide.

In slowing real estate markets, many agents arrange fancy prizes to raffle off at the open houses held for real estate professionals—perhaps a week's vacation in Puerto Vallarta—and even fancier prizes for those who bring in an acceptable offer to purchase. Sometimes this works, sometimes it does not. My own suggestion is that you decide on a relatively simple trademark prize, something that people associate with you and give that out at open houses. A fine pen, a good appointment book, a copy of the book you're now reading, a subscription to a magazine, perhaps. Or, if you have an agreement with a restaurant to co-op on certain promotional efforts, a pair of dinners there would be a good prize. Or, if you love music, a compact disc might be a good prize. The possibilities are endless.

As for the prize to be awarded to the person bringing in an accepted offer to purchase—my own experience is that this does very little to get a home sold. Real estate professionals do not generally manipulate people into buying a specific property, especially if they want a long and happy career in real estate. They help their clients find the home that works best for them, and if that happens to be a home with such a prize attached to it, it's sheer happenstance…and the prize should doubtless go to the buyer, not to the real estate professional. Bottom line, in any case—this has very little effect regarding the sale of the property.

The point, after all, is to get (1) real estate professionals excited about a property, resulting in (2) many visits from their clients. You will have your own clients as well and, in hot markets, you may sell from an open house. (In cool markets, the sale of an open house is about as likely as winning $1,000 in the local lottery—only slightly lower than the odds of selling the home to someone who calls about a classified ad for the property.)

Every Property Has a Story

The real estate industry is very gradually moving from left-brain, fact-laden promotional items—like the flyers that tell you how many bedrooms, how many baths, and how much square footage—and learning the value of story. But only very gradually. We aren't accustomed to thinking this way. We still think too much like the guy on television who loudly lists the features of the cars he has for sale on his used car lot. It's time to move beyond this.

I have suggested you create a brochure or flyer, an in-house guide, and open house postcards. Here are the steps I advise you to take.

When you meet with the sellers, you might want to store an unopened bottle of wine in your car and ask the sellers if they would be willing to tell you the story of their house over wine. If they don't drink wine, perhaps you could have some premium soft drinks in the car as well.

After you have found out what they want to accomplish by selling their home, have toured the house, have gone through the review of recent comparable sales, and have shown them what specifically will be involved in your marketing plan for their home—after, indeed, they have signed a listing with you (or before, if the home is already listed by your office associate and this is your "pretend" listing)—lighten things up with wine or a soft drink, ask leading questions, and listen deeply and carefully to the story of their experience of this house, taking notes.

The same night, write a story about the house—not the story of the current owners' experience of the house, but a bit of pertinent fiction about how the buyers of the home will enjoy living in it. Include details of the house's construction, talk about as many of the pertinent features and amenities as you can, wrap it all up in a story—perhaps the story of someone coming home from work, stopping at a special store on the way home for fresh produce or dessert, feeling the pressures of the workday evaporate.

This is, it turns out, one of the most effective possible ways to write about and advertise a home. Even if the people you imagine as the next owners of the house don't entirely resemble the future owners, everyone who reads this brochure will be drawn in and will remember the house well. And by the way, if you don't feel up to writing the story, take the notes and give them to an assistant who can.

Many astute real estate professionals have realized that dressing up a home so that it shows well—the term for this is "staging a home"—not only makes a home sell faster than it otherwise would but also generally brings in a better price for the home than it otherwise would have received (and this, ideally, will be a part of your conceptual bag of tricks as a master lister/marketer). Creating a story for the home works in a similar way. It feeds the imagination of the potential buyer, draws him and her into the home, creates an invitation for the buyer to make the home his and her own. Similarly, just as a well-decorated house may bring in top dollar from a buyer who then completely remodels the home—a counter-intuitive fact of life in real estate—the story you create may involve a family of four and yet completely seduce a family of two.

Your story will probably have a central theme—the calm provided by the remodeled bathroom and outdoor hot tub, for example. Thus, your marketing of each home is likely to have something like a theme.

You'll want to be sure that the theme doesn't limit the uses of the house, but does give those who see the house something of a "handle" to help them remember it and to focus them on the brochure's story.

The in-house guide can simply take the potential buyers through the house, much like a scripted explanation you'd hear on the little headphone devices in museums. (Sort of brings to mind my first story record, on which Hopalong Cassidy reminded the reader to turn the page when he jingled his spurs. "Turn left into the dining room when I say the word.") The point is that you are, indeed, scripting the showing of the house, anticipating many questions that might be asked, but not treading on the toes of the real estate professional who is actually showing the house to people. (Indeed, the in-house guide is probably even more important as a script for the professionals doing that showing than for the buyers doing the looking. For that reason, you'll want to print plenty of them and be certain real estate professionals take one when they come to preview the home.

What is accomplished by all of this?

Several things, most of them obvious:

- The home will sell more quickly and at a good price.

- You'll probably end up showing properties to many new clients, very likely leading to your first home sales.

- People who see how you market a home are likely to want to have you do similar work for them, leading perhaps to your first listings.

- It will be something of a coming-out party for you in your profession, as other real estate professionals learn who you are and how you work. They are likely to see you as a force to be reckoned with, which is not a bad thing at all.

Then what?

Once the home sells, find another. Keep at it until you have listings of your own and/or so many clients that you really don't have time to help others sell their listings. (By the way, the second time through, you might want to ask a percentage of the sales commission for the work that you do. And you might want to hold on to that title, "Manager of Marketing." It will keep you from looking too much like dangerous competition to your peers.)

CHAPTER THIRTY-THREE

Yikes! My Phone Is Starting To Ring!

Throughout the time that you are jump-starting your career (see the chapter above), you will also be launching your marketing program and, in a short while, that program will start bringing in new clients. Indeed, the ingredients of your jump-starting are very much a part of your overall marketing strategy. You should continue to distribute the brochures and/or flyers you make for each of your listings, along with the invitations to open houses.

There should be a powerful synergism to all the ingredients in your marketing program. The newsletter, of course, will be far more powerful if something else you are doing—like sending out a brochure for a listing—catches people's attention, causing them to read your newsletter each time you send it out.

And then comes the day when your phone begins to ring. I can only give three crucial pieces of advice:

▶ 1. Have your listing presentation and the elements in your customizable marketing program for houses clearly established so that you can talk about them with ease. We've already looked at the basics of such a presentation. You would be wise to create a notebook with examples of brochures and flyers you've done, with copies of in-house guides, with postcards and testimonials from clients—all done up neatly in plastic pages.

▶ 2. Prepare an approach to dealing with potential buyers for the first time. I will admit that my left brain, which does occasionally make itself known—but not often—likes the idea of sitting down with people and asking them a long list of questions before taking them to see any houses. You need to go far deeper than the usual stuff about how many bedrooms and square feet. You need to know how people actually want to live in their house, so that you can match their needs to the homes currently on the market and come up with a home that's a fit.

However, I rarely did it this way myself. When someone comes in to look at a house, she isn't usually in the mood for lengthy, semi-rational conversations. She doesn't want to be interviewed. He and/or she usually want to get in the car and look at the house they called to inquire about—whether a house they read about in a classified ad or a house they saw while driving around local neighborhoods.

So take them. Ask them a bunch of questions while you're driving them to the house. Watch their responses very closely as they look at the house in question. If you feel inspired, take them to see another, and another.

Then it's time to sit down and talk, perhaps over coffee or tea. Time to build a relationship, to increase trust, and to find out what makes these people tick and what sort of a house will really support the way they love to live. A lot of questions built on things you noticed are a great idea—"I noticed you liked the fact that the house wasn't connected directly to the garage—can you tell me about that?" This sort of question shows you're paying attention to their needs and responses, and opens the door for further insights into the house they'll want to live in.

I have known a great many fine real estate professionals who give their new buyer clients a form to fill out ("How many bedrooms are you seeking?" etc.). I don't think they set up a good relationship at the level where the rubber meets the road when you're looking for a home—inevitably, a rather emotional level for most (but not all) people. What you really want at the outset is a chance to observe these people looking at a house or two or three, then it's time to ask a bunch of questions and build up a relationship that will allow them to trust you and tell you just what it is they desire, even when what they desire embarrasses them or worries them (probably because of the potential cost) and they're reticent to talk about it.

▶ 3. Make sure your assistant is up and running, able to handle much of your marketing program and other related research and work. Your business may pick up rather quickly, and your extra time may all but vanish as a result.

▶ 4. Make sure your friends and family realize that your life may soon change radically. I called it the "explosion factor" because it is possible to get a phone call from a client in the middle of dinner. "Sorry to bother you now, but we found out we have to make an offer tonight on that house." Often, you will have to excuse yourself and get to work.

Further, you'll want to hold open houses on the weekend, and this may radically change the patterns of activities for your whole family. Draw you family and friends into a kind of partnership of understanding with you and thank them constantly for their support.

Setting Boundaries

Having said this, I must add that you will constantly need to set boundaries. Often, when people are making huge, life-changing decisions, they assume that they can call at any hour of the day or night for advice and even for consolation. My first sale involved a man who worried ceaselessly about his pending purchase, calling me at 10:30 or 11:00 at night and bellowing, "Bill! Tell me again that I made the right decision! Please!" I told him, again and again. But this routine was nearly abusive. Today, I would suggest that he take a quick drink of brandy and call me in the morning. They don't call me Dr. Fisher for nothing.

Similarly, though you hold open houses on the weekends (unless religious reasons forbid it for you), your open house doesn't need to remain open into the evening. Make a big deal of your open house in the afternoon, and close everything down at a specified time. No surprises. You're outta there—unless (explosion) you happen to be writing up an offer. All of which leads us to…

▶ 5. Never forget that you are doing this work, in part, so that you can support all the things you and each member of your family find meaningful, worthwhile and important in life. More on this in our final chapters.

PART SIX

I Am Not (Just) A Real Estate Career, And Life Is A Beautiful Adventure

CHAPTER THIRTY-FOUR

FAQs

Service-Oriented Marketing—once you get a feeling for it and once you realize that many businesses have been using these principles in their marketing for a long time and have been revolutionizing their marketing programs in the process—begins to make sense and to seem almost obvious and very nearly old-fashioned. We're all experts, yes?

But questions remain, many of them arising from the assumptions behind genuinely old-fashioned ways of marketing ourselves as real estate professionals. Most of us still have a knee-jerk need for our marketing effort to bring in a listing or a sale as quickly as possible—not a bad wish, but rarely the right first requirement on our marketing program. Why? **Because we're replacing the need for tomorrow's deal with the desire for a long-term career, and our marketing efforts quickly begin to reflect that change in attitudes and assumptions.**

Let's amble through several of the questions that still arise from time to time, noticing that it's only natural for them to bubble up from the tar pits of our industry's past. Much of what we'll discuss here has been touched on elsewhere in the book, but experience tells me that many people will still need a fuller answer to these questions.

Question #1: Does service-oriented marketing work for everyone?

This question needs a context. Many years ago I was the manager of a fairly large real estate office and I can assure you that many of the people in the office believed fervently that these principles and these marketing techniques didn't work for them. Others were simply too impatient; they wanted to put together a big deal...now. Others had such "Type A" personalities that they just couldn't sit still long enough to mess with marketing programs, with newsletters, with anything but the fastest path to another deal.

I am not putting these people down. But I do want to make this clarification of the question above. First—yes, service-oriented marketing works for everyone. Second—it only really works for people who are at home with it, who are fully invested in and identified with the marketing materials they are using, and who tend to think in Big Picture terms...about their career, more than about today's lunch.

Many people are simply not constitutionally endowed with the personality and character that will ever be at home with service-oriented marketing. They will rush to get behind the next provider of leads, too impatient to concern themselves with the question of how dangerous those leads may be to their career (because they involve potentially incompatible clients and could result in unpleasant transactions and lots of bad comments on their performance).

Obviously, the writer of this book is very much at home with service-oriented marketing. I have to admit to being biased in its favor. But my point is simple. It takes a lot of different kinds of animals to make up a wild and healthy zoo, and some of them just won't get excited about this kind of marketing.

This raises a very important point.

Question #1a: "What if everyone sent out newsletters and similar marketing pieces? How would my marketing program work then?"

The answer, of course, is that your marketing program probably wouldn't work all that well if every real estate professional were sending out similar items. I mean, in California alone, there are half a million homo sapiens licensed to practice real estate. That could mean an avalanche of newsletters.

But of course, this won't happen. We've already seen the reason. Not that many people have the patience for service-oriented marketing and sending out carefully-prepared marketing pieces. How many creative, helpful, interesting marketing pieces do you get a month? It's probably a remarkably small number—especially remarkable because this form of marketing is so successful for those who get fully behind it—and the number will almost certainly remain very small.

Sadly, it's much like the issue of truly superior service. How many businesses provide it? It's a minority, even though nearly everyone is inclined to stick like super glue to a company or a professional advisor who can be relied on to provide great service. Most people in business just don't want to be bothered with the extra steps, the unexpected acts of kindness, the constant parade of extra miles that a great provider of service goes.

But this raises another point: One of the main reasons you can rely on a good service-oriented marketing program to help you build a great career is that few people in your profession will be marketing themselves in this way. You will stand out. You will look like the most active, competent, experienced, knowledgeable, caring person in the local marketplace. Indeed, you will look like someone who is not quite in the same profession as everyone else—just as Trader Joe's looks like something rather different from any other food market and Cirque du Soleil doesn't quite look like what we used to think of as a circus. Both stand alone in otherwise crowded fields.

Again, this makes us wonder why more people don't go at service-oriented marketing 150%. But they don't...and not many will.

Question #2: I'm a business person and I want to be able to measure the success of my marketing program. Exactly how can I do that with a service-oriented marketing program?"

This is an important question. No one wants to develop a marketing program that doesn't bring in any business, and then to keep on throwing money into the program because there seems to be no way to measure its success.

But there is a caveat—as you doubtless know by now. If you are marketing primarily to build and nourish a career, rather than marketing primarily to bring in tomorrow's transaction, you will need to measure the effectiveness of your marketing in non-traditional ways. (The old saying about giving a man a fish vs. teaching the man to fish comes to mind here.)

Measuring Success

Yes, it's still good to know how many phone calls your program is generating, and how many listings, and how many sales. But there are other factors that are equally important.

- Can you sense that people in your target market are becoming more aware of you and, further, that they are beginning to recognize your abilities as a professional? (Think, for example, of the people whispering, as I entered a local restaurant, "That's the Village San Juan Specialist!" Hey—my name wasn't exactly in lights on the theater marquee, but I was attaining a healthy kind of gentle fame...a positive reputation.)

- Are you beginning to hear from potential clients, calling for your assistance?

- Are the majority of people you hear from "warm" or compatible potential clients who are inclined to trust you and to allow you to do your best work for them?

- Are the numbers of unexpected referrals increasing?

- Are your marketing materials getting praise from the people who receive them?

These are not scientific ways of measuring the exact success of your marketing—but there is no such science. What's important is to stay attentive to why your clients call on you and whether they are usually "warm." It is equally important to remain mindful of the quality of your business, and not just the quantity.

Question #3: "Big newsletters may be interesting, but my people don't want a lot to read. They want something no longer than one page that they can down in a minute or two."

This isn't exactly a question; it's an assertion. And I've heard it many times.

The first thing to worry about is the term, "my people." Who are "my people"? What makes them "my people"?

I would argue—and this is far more important than most people imagine—that they are not "your people" at all. Many of the real estate agents who refer to their clients and potential clients in this way are only a short distance from the error my friend made, calling all his clients "assholes." Stop with the generalizations. Allow these people to be who they are, every one of them unique.

But enough of my soap box lecture. The next point, already made in these pages, is that a large number of studies have been done on the relative effectiveness of marketing pieces long and short...and the longs have it by a mile.

A longer letter allows you to develop a relationship with the reader, and that relationship continues to build, month after month. A short letter makes a small impression. It doesn't last. It isn't effective.

The implied question here (something like, "Why do you suggest sending out a 4-page newsletter when I myself don't have the patience to read that much in one sitting?") relates closely to another question...

Question #4: "Yeah, but I don't want to bug people with my marketing stuff very often, so wouldn't it be better to limit my mailing to once every three months?

As I've said before, **if your marketing materials "bug" those who receive them, then you'd better go back to the drawing board and design better marketing materials.** I will be dogmatic about this. We're accustomed to advertising—"Interruption Advertising" from commercial breaks on television to telephone calls in the middle of dinner—that is almost always irritating. We've even come to believe that irritation and annoyance are two of the necessary features of advertising, perhaps thinking that we won't get people's attention if we don't shout at them or make them angry. Almost all advertising has moved beyond these archaic ideas (other than, of course, the guy selling used cars on television every Saturday morning and late into the night). It doesn't work, it leads people to dislike you and feel abused by you, and it fulfills none of the aims of service-oriented marketing.

As a result, you want to send the right marketing materials to the right people—people who will appreciate and enjoy what you send, people who will look forward to what you send them.

Once every three months is simply not enough. The decision to buy a home and the decision to sell a home both have a lengthy period of gestation. Buyers and sellers today do a lot of research, largely on the Internet, and a lot of talking—to their spouses or partners, to their family and friends, to their business associates. And when they decide to buy or sell, they usually start working with a real estate professional very quickly, making the decision within three days.

If you're only dropping into their consciousness once every three months, you're not providing the service, frankly, that you should be providing someone who is preparing to buy or sell. You're not sending out information; you're not offering to serve them; you're not helping them with their research; you're not "with them," so to speak, as they go through this rather intense process.

There's another very important point to be made here. Most of us, when we go through all the trouble of creating and mailing out a marketing piece, feel that we have done a Very Big Thing (VBT), and that everyone who receives this VBT should be highly impressed, should respond, should ask you to come by and list their home pronto.

It just doesn't work that way. Remember: You have to run a new television advertisement by the normal guy about two dozen times before he is even aware of what is being advertised. This is a tough fact of life to deal with. It's one of the reasons that so many people just don't want to be bothered with a service-oriented marketing program. The mere possibility that the VBT they send out to their target market could wind up in the circular file without even being read is a bitter pill, indeed. So they'd rather hold another open house, drop their line into the pond, and hope for a good nibble.

Tempting, yes. But it's not the way to build a career as efficiently and effectively as possible.

So get at least one marketing piece out to your target market every month. Let me stress that word: EVERY month. Even the act of getting it out at nearly the same time each month tells your potential clients that you are trustworthy, timely and reliable.

Go for it!

Question #5: "Yeah, but I can't really afford to send out 1,000 newsletters every month to the same group of people. How about if I send out

500 one month to one group and 500 the next month to the other group?"

If you can't afford 1,000 newsletters, send out as many as you can afford. But send them to the same people, month after month. There may be some curious mathematical sense in which it seems a good idea to send 500 here one month, 500 there the next—as if you were plowing a larger field than you otherwise could—but issues of quality quickly overtake issues of quantity when it comes to marketing.

In short, start with a core target market and give everyone in the market all the goods you have…the whole program. As your business and income expand, you can expand the number of people you're sending newsletters to—or whatever you're sending them.

Question #5a: "What if I'm just starting in this area and I really don't have more than about 125 people on my mailing list?"

I suggest you print 200 newsletters. Send 125 to your target market. Leave the rest at very appropriate places, like…

- A local espresso stand whose owner you've worked up a cooperative deal with: they put your newsletter on their counter and you buy a free latte for anyone using the coupon in your newsletter.

- A local restaurant—similar deal.

- A church or club or other organization you are affiliated with.

- Open houses you hold. Listing presentations you make.

And you will want to carry a dozen or so copies of the letter so that you can hand it out to people you encounter.

CHAPTER THIRTY-FIVE

Taking It A Little Deeper

I suggested that you develop what is essentially a rough script for your ideal transaction—a pattern of events that is always inspired by the desire to create a successful, fulfilling career, not just to race to this one commission check. It's even more important, though we enter a rather tricky realm here, to develop a positive attitude toward your work and your ability to succeed. In short, it's crucial to know that real estate is something you can do, that you can provide people with genuine, invaluable support, and that everything you do to attract clients works according to your positive intentions.

Now, we might call this the "woo-woo" chapter, I suppose—a little Positive Thinking Cocktail, some chicken soup for the successful Realtor®'s soul. Call it whatever you like. It is very important and utterly real.

You will not have a fulfilling career in real estate if you don't believe you can.

In fact, you need to *know* you can. You need to know this is something you are capable of. You need to know that you can bring great value to people's transactions. You need to know you deserve a profound level of trust. You need to know that you deserve every penny of your commission for the work that you do.

A friend of mine, a real estate professional who is also a professional worrier, constantly demonstrates the truth of what I am saying here. He is very gradually becoming a service-oriented marketer. Ironically, every time he adds something to his marketing program, he worries that it won't work. And guess what—his worry proves his fears are correct.

The phone rings and I pick it up. "This isn't working for me," he tells me before I have a chance to say hello. "It may work for your other clients but it isn't working for me."

We talk for a while. He has recently decided to send 1,500 newsletters out to a specific target market every month. His worrying mind is certain this is going to cost him more than the added income it will bring in. He's only sent out one set of newsletters to all 1,500 potential clients so far.

"Have you heard anything in response?" I ask.

"Nothing," he declares. "Not a darn thing. Nothing."

"No one mentioned the newsletter?"

"Oh—well—yeah," he admits. "I've run into a few people who said they liked it."

"Yes?"

"But they didn't ask me to list their house or help them buy something," he almost snarled.

"Maybe none of them is ready to buy or sell a house," I suggested.

"Well, obviously!" he said, impatient. "Why do I need to hear from people who don't want to buy or sell real estate?"

"My friend," I suggest, "take a deep breath. You're not thinking very clearly."

"Oh," he says. "Yeah. I guess you're right."

"You want to hear from these people because, number one, you want to get to know your future clients and, number two, you know that someday they'll be wanting to buy or sell real estate."

"And in the meantime," my friend adds, "they might have an Uncle Herbie who wants to buy a home in this area."

"Now you're talking."

"Boy," my friend sighs, "sometimes I get obsessed with the half-empty glass of water."

"Sometimes you do. But those times are becoming less and less frequent."

"Yeah," he concludes breathlessly. "Well, gotta go. My one o'clock appointment just walked into the office."

"Have a good time," I say, and I can feel the transformation already taking place in my friend. Placed in front of actual clients, he becomes who he is and leaves the worry behind. He does the work that needs to be done; he listens deeply; he explains clearly. His clients love him dearly.

Back to the point at hand, in any case: If your service-oriented marketing is to work for you, you must...

> • Know that it will;
>
> • Know that you're providing a great service with your marketing materials;
>
> • Know that you are fully capable of providing the kind of experience those who respond to your marketing hope for and expect;
>
> • Know that this is going to be another good day in your life.

Which leads us to another extremely crucial point...

CHAPTER THIRTY-SIX
You Are Not A House; You Are Not A Real Estate Career; You Are A Richly Complex And Fascinating Human Being

Right in the heart of Florence, Italy—not far from the Piazza del Duomo where the heartbeat of artistic and architectural geniuses like Giotto and Brunelleschi can still be heard gently pulsing above the sound of today's traffic and tourists—you will find a gelato shop with the irresistible name, *Perché No?* Why not, indeed?

Why not indulge yourself in one of the great pleasures to be found on this planet, ice cream confections that make your taste buds stand up and do the funky chicken, the bump, the brazen boogaloo? This is a taste of heaven on earth.

Perché No, with its broad array of surprising flavors ranging from exotic chocolates to fruits like honeydew and kiwi, has been selling its gelati for a long time. I first ventured into the shop, google-eyed and drooling at all I saw, in 1963, when I was a student at Stanford University's Florence campus. When I returned in about 1993, tears of recognition in my eyes, it was still there, though its surroundings had grown a good deal more upscale in the intervening years.

When you visit Florence, seek it out and please, let me know if it's still there. If not, you will doubtless find even better gelati in some unexpected places. A little shop in the cathedral piazza in the wonderful hill town of Orvieto, last time I visited, for example, knocked my socks off with its fruit flavors.

Indeed, when you travel through Italy, you may want to do a personal survey of the gelati offered here and there. While you're at it, you may want to do a survey of the different versions of tiramisu to be found in different corners of the country.

Every one of us probably has favorite places, cherished memories, and adventures we're waiting to visit or revisit. Life, as I have learned from some of my greatest teachers, young and old, is a banquet—an embarrassment of riches. This is not to deny that we do experience pain, traumas and depressions. Nor is it to assert that gelato can solve all of life's problems (though it does go some distance toward a remedy for many irritations, particularly boredom and fast food).

The point I would make here—and I want to make it with all the delicacy, subtlety and gentleness of a sledge hammer—is that your real estate career must support a wonderful life. It must support all those moments at the baseball field when you watch your son or daughter developing into a capable, enthusiastic athlete; all those evenings out with your spouse when you unwind in a fine local restaurant; all those long hours alone as you work at hobbies that breathe life into your heart and soul. It must...and that means you must never set aside what you love about being alive. Nothing is more important.

You are not a real estate career. As long as that is true, you can remain someone who finds great enjoyment and satisfaction in assisting people with real estate questions and transactions, helping to make people's lives work a bit better, being at the heart of the huge decisions that bring meaning and richness to people's lives.

Since you are not a real estate career, since you are someone who, in his or her business life, is a highly respected professional, you will want to—need to, have to—establish meaningful boundaries. After making my first sale, as I mentioned, I received phone calls from my client, the homebuyer, nearly every night until escrow closed. Remember him?— the guy who wanted me to assure him nightly that he'd put together a good deal and wouldn't lose his shirt because he'd bought a $93,000 house?

It wasn't until a bit later in my career that I realized I didn't have to interrupt everything I was doing, including sleep, to coddle this likable worry wart. I was just keeping the fires of his worry alive by taking him so seriously. It would have been far better to tell him, the first time he called, that I was off-duty—reading, sleeping, spending time with my wife—but that I'd be back on-duty the next morning, and he could call then. (Which, of course, he wouldn't do, because he would be back on-duty as well, and would probably have slept through his night jitters better, knowing that I really wasn't worried about his transaction.)

One of the most difficult things about real estate is that, like the care and feeding of very active children, all that you do as a real estate professional can sop up every available moment of your time and every bit of your energy, and then some. But it doesn't need to. Instead, you need to make clear (to yourself, primarily) that there are things you will do and things you won't do. You won't wake up from a needed night's sleep to hold the hand of an unnecessarily worrying client, for example.

You can see the suppressed frustration in your fellow real estate agents, as a matter of fact. The inner rage at being at the beck and call of so many people makes many agents bristle if a fellow agent asks a simple favor, and also causes them to treat ancillary service providers—title insurance company representatives, for example–very poorly.

A Balanced Life

▶ **One:** It's important to review your boundaries constantly, knowing that you will occasionally have to break through them—if, for example, a transaction is in tremendous jeopardy and requires action on your part...even though you're in the middle of your dinner. But remember: break through your boundaries as seldom as possible. Ideally, never.

▶ **Two:** It's also important—crucial—to remember the bottom line reason you're doing all the work that you do as a real estate professional. You're doing it because you want to live a full and rich life. You want to assist people in matters that are very important to them. You want to earn the trust of your clients and develop great working relationships and, sometimes, friendships. You want to be a positive force in your community, especially in your "target market." You want to be able to afford an occasional trip to advance your research of Italian gelati, Northern California wineries, Hawaiian surfing beaches, international jazz festivals—or whatever turns on your headlamps. You want to be able to send children to camp, to good schools, to fine colleges. You want to be able to stay active, healthy, glad to be alive. You want to delve deeply into your primary relationships, with wife, partner, friends, family. You want to nourish and expand your work in hobbies that delight you. You want to involve yourself in organizations that support your passions and interests and beliefs.

You want, in short, a very full life. If you don't make sure you have that full life, your career will suffer greatly. You'll have one-dimensional relationships with three-dimensional clients. You'll have few opportunities to meet people and expand your client base. You may just end up like Joe Doakes, whom we encountered early in this book, spending your days with a huge thermos of coffee, sitting at a metal desk in an empty office, waiting for the phone to ring, no longer even knowing all that he's missing.

▶ **Three:** It's very important to write personal and family and community activities into your schedule in ink, making sure those dates and times remain every bit as important as the business appointments you have.

Give yourself regular time each day for some exercise. Don't wait for failing health to warn you that either you use it or you lose it. (I speak from experience here.)

Give yourself time for church or whatever activity feeds your spirit, and that could include a weekly walk in this hills or on the beach, a time when you look again and again at the miraculous face of wonder all around you.

Give yourself time for the hobbies that matter to you. If you love to read, do so—and go as often as possible to a monthly reading group. If you love to make music, do so. If you love to listen to music, to study art, to play tennis, to run in marathons, to help at the food bank, or to meditate for an hour each day, do so. Doing these things can be far more important to you, in the long run, than earning an extra bit of income.

I know a retired plumber, a very good fellow with a "Type A" personality who can't sit still long enough to read a book. He noticed a few things about my life that he found attractive and we fell into long conversations in which he'd swear to me that he has never found anything in his life that he is truly interested in. Nothing, he said, really revs his internal motors. He misses his work, he claimed, not because he liked it, but because it gave him things he had to do.

Afternoon conversations that heated up around the subject of politics, that grew excited around matters of history, that began to leap and bound around the problems of designing furniture and additions to houses—all told me that his lack of interest in any earthly thing was a bunch of nonsense. What he lacked, thanks to very abusive parents, was simple self-esteem. He didn't believe, down in the murky confusion of his subconscious mind, that he had any right to assert his own preferences and name his own likes and dislikes.

Thankfully, this is passing. He's doing a lot of work in the community, both for pay and for free; he's studying the history of economics; he's doing a lot with his daughter and grandchildren. He's a late bloomer in the extreme, but he's very much alive.

Those of us who are not inclined by nature to assert our own needs over the needs of others can fall into my friend's trap. It was a very nearly suicidal path he was following. We need to do what we love to do, give what we are most capable of giving, and experience that what we give is of value to our family, our friends and our clients.

Doing so, we will live full lives in this great and varied planetary banquet. Not doing so will likely mean that we burn out in our professional and our personal lives and become very ill.

And if those are the choices, it shouldn't be difficult to make the right choice—but it often is. So…

▶ **Four:** Figure out approximately how much money you will need to live the life you want and to provide your family with the life you want to provide. Be conservative. You don't have to chase after wealth when you simply have enough for the things you truly love.

One of the greatest traps in a real estate career hides in the fact that, if you market yourself successfully and develop good professional skills, you are likely to wake up one day and notice that it's possible to make more money than you ever imagined making. Your mind reels. Yow! Look at all the money you could make if you spent your time doing nothing but real estate! Your relationship with your partner or spouse can wait, right? Postpone that exercise regime. Forget those jazz festivals. Apply yourself strictly to your real estate work, and then… someday, off in the future, everyone in your family will thank you for all the money you've earned, and how secure you all feel, and how you can do just about anything you can imagine wanting to do.

This is the Big Lie in the life of a person who is paid with commissions. The sky's the limit. That's true. But if you race toward the sun—like the mythic figure named Icarus who flew with wings of wax—you will burn out and fall back to the earth.

Remember: you are developing and nourishing a real estate CAREER, a professional life that will last a good many years, bringing in the cash flow you need and creating the opportunities you desire. You don't need to be a superstar, whatever that may be. You simply need to make the money your careful analysis has determined will bring you and your family all that you desire. You simply need to do the work that will bring in that amount of money. You don't need to work 24/7. You don't need to miss out on the lives of your children. You don't need to pass on that wonderful trip to Cancun. You don't need to throw a cold blanket over your passion for Mozart.

You need, instead, to feel as alive as you possibly can—healthy, fulfilled, relatively secure, excited by all you are doing and experiencing.

That's the bottom line. Indeed, you may wish to form a Bottom Line Club in your office—a group of colleagues who go out to lunch once a week and talk about the ways they're keeping their careers and lives in perspective, and keeping themselves very much alive.

I happened to call one of my newsletter clients on his 60th birthday not long ago. He'd been using a newsletter I write—building and bracing his career with precisely the service-oriented marketing we've looked at in this book—for over twenty years, and he was feeling gently philosophical on his birthday.

"It's been good," he said. "I've made a lot of money, and had a lot of fun." I could hear children in the background. The party was only beginning. His family had come to celebrate him in his office before taking him home to a big birthday party.

"I expect it will be good for as many more years as I'm in this business, too," he added, then he admitted he had to go or he'd get in trouble with his grandson.

I can only say that it has been good for me as well. The work I've done with my colleagues has been valuable to hundreds of fine real estate careers. I hope this book, which summarizes most of what we've learned over a quarter of a century, will help hundreds more—especially you.

PART SEVEN

A New Framework

CHAPTER THIRTY-SEVEN
Imagining Radical Changes to our Real Estate Practice

It was 4:30, a quiet afternoon, and I was gathering my 'Open House' materials and preparing to leave when an elderly man, perhaps in his mid-70s, with wild silver hair like a crazed halo around his head and eyebrows like shrubs above his eyes, entered the house. He walked with a white cane and carried an old leather briefcase, and, though his clothes seemed to have been pulled from the bargain pile at a local consignment shop, there was something rather sporty about the way he looked, as if he could bounce right into a Fred Astaire impression. Maybe it was that cane.

"Am I too late?" he asked, breathing a bit heavily.

"Please," I responded. "Come in." I wanted to get home, but the old guy made me curious. This was a very large home. Could he really be interested in buying it?

"I'm probably a waste of your time," he said, bowing slightly. "I'm not a buyer, you know."

"I doubt that you could waste my time," I said, not quite knowing why I said that, but believing it nonetheless.

"Oh, I probably could," he laughed, "but I really don't intend to. It's just—I'm interested in your business ideas." He reached out his hand. "I'm Eldred Frame."

"Pleased to meet you, sir." His handshake was strong.

"My nephew Nick is selling this house—you know Nick, of course. He's sent me all the materials you've put together to market this home, and I have to say, I'm deeply impressed."

"Thank you," I said.

"Can we sit and talk for a little while?" Eldred asked.

"Of course," I responded, and we sat in his nephew's living room.

"Nice place Nick's got here," Eldred commented.

"Very nice."

"Well," Eldred began, "here's the thing. I've also read your book—that *You Are Not A House* thing. Cute title, by the way."

"Thanks."

"Look, Bill, I'll level with you. Okay?"

I was puzzled, but I said it was fine with me.

"Okay. Here's what I want to start with: I don't think your book goes far enough. I don't think your own practice goes far enough, either."

"In what way?"

"You like sausages?" he asked.

"I suppose I do," I responded, now completely baffled.

"I'm a butcher. In my business, they call me 'the scientist' because I study every aspect of my product, from taste to nutritional value to pricing to marketing, etc. And I developed a line of sausages that make people swoon. I mean it. People love my sausages. They come from miles to buy them."

"Good."

"Good?" he laughed. "Here's the good part. How do you let people know that you are selling sausages that are several grades above what they can get anywhere else? Answer me that, Bill."

"Good marketing," I responded. "Informational marketing. Free samples, too, I suspect. And word-of-mouth referrals."

"Okay," he said. "Good enough, maybe. What am I trying to do with my marketing?"

"You're probably trying to suggest to people that your sausages are the best on the market," I said.

"Bingo!" Eldred Frame yelled. "You're exactly wrong!" He smiled at me. "To repeat, my friend: My sausages are several levels above any others on the market. What I am saying here is that they're in a class by themselves, not that they'll win in any taste tests you might have.

These sausages are an experience unto themselves. They don't have to compete with any other sausages. Do you start to get my point?"

"I don't think so, Mr. Frame."

"But you will," he said, smiling again. "I know you will. What I needed to do was to present my sausages as an entirely new experience— not as just another set of sausages that was better than the others. So I called them "Enlightenment Sausages." I developed casings and wrappers that would keep them extremely fresh. I packaged them in such a way that they spark the curiosity. I mean, what could these be in such a beautiful package, covered with lines of ancient love poetry and drawings of graceful meadows? And I sold them—ready?—in gourmet food stores. Didn't even carry them in my own meat shop. Got it so far?"

"I think so."

"Okay. I developed systems for producing these sausages, because demand began to grow very, very fast. I hired people who specialized in certain areas of production, shipping and marketing. Remember, Bill—we're talking sausages here, not exotic ice cream or shade-grown coffee beans. Sausages."

"Yes?"

"Bill, I became a millionaire—not that becoming a millionaire is the point of my story. The point is that I found out there is a different way of creating and marketing, one that gets outside of the box, as they say, and truly works. It does wonderful things. It creates success, it gets a very good set of products out to the people who will appreciate them the most, it brings pleasure to people's lives, it reduces the amount that we preoccupy ourselves with competition in our businesses, it even seems to me to get closer to the way your brain and your emotions and your spirit come together when you create something good. Are you hearing me?"

"I certainly am."

"I knew you would," he said, and again he smiled. "Listen. One of the first things I want you to do is to read *Blue Ocean Strategy* by W. Chan Kim and Renée Mauborgne. Really provocative book. The basic ideas are pretty simple but it's simple ideas like this that can totally revolutionize your life."

"Let me write that down," I said.

"Better yet," said the old man, "I'll give you a copy. I have extras." And he pulled a book out of the briefcase at his feet.

"Thanks," I said.

"Now here's why I rode the train all the way here from Jersey," he continued. "I can't fly, by the way. Scares me to death."

I chuckled.

"Someday maybe I'll tell you why," he added. "But let's get to the point. I believe there are quite a few people doing something like what I've done, each in his and her own way—developing products and services that just stand out as something new and different and valuable in the marketplace. They don't need to compete with others because there really aren't any others out there doing quite what they're doing. They just need to make sure the market for their work is aware of what they've done. Remember, Bill, not everyone will like what they've created…but there is a very strong target market for what they've done, and they want to get to those people."

"How do they do it?" I asked.

"Precisely through the kind of marketing you have written about. You are exactly on the right track, but you don't really follow through on the difference that takes place when you fully realize that you're not fighting your way to the top of an existing market. You're making a new one."

"I think I follow that," I said.

"Good!" he said. "We're talking about the Starbucks that revolutionizes the sale of coffee, the Cirque du Soleil that creates an uncanny combination of circus and theater and it results in a whole new form of entertainment, the iPod that develops a new way of doing what the Walkman used to do. That kind of thing."

"Okay," I said, warming up to his infectious enthusiasm.

"Okay, indeed," he responded. "Now answer me this: Who in real estate has done this kind of thing? I mean, can you point out one company, or even one person, who has truly created an utterly new form of real estate practice?"

I thought for a moment. "Maybe the company that built an office whose agents pay a desk fee and receive 100% of their commission."

"Nonsense!" Mr. Frame sputtered. "A good idea, I admit, but not a revolution. I mean, what does that do for the public's experience of buying and selling a house?"

"Nothing," I admitted.

"Okay, we could quibble, maybe. We could say that this created a small change in the way people practice real estate. But it isn't like a Southwest Airlines or a Jet Blue, transforming the way we fly, am I right?"

"You are."

"I want to share my thinking with you under two categories, Bill," he said. "The first is logistics. The second is adventure."

"Adventure?" I asked.

"Hold on," he laughed. "We'll get there. First let me pose a few questions and make a few suggestions about the logistics involved in helping people buy and sell homes."

"I'm all ears," I said.

"I've studied this for a few years because, and here's the bottom line, I want to build a real estate company that completely changes the face of real estate for all time."

"Wow," I said. "That's no small order."

"The whole enchilada," Eldred Frame agreed.

"With maybe a sausage thrown in for good measure."

"Right. Can I go on?"

"Please."

"Imagine with me a relatively small company made up of the following people. First, you have two people who work the office. They are extremely high-class secretaries, receptionists, assistants and in some instances, back-up real estate agents. They have licenses. They could sell real estate if they wanted, and they can receive a percentage of commissions. They can also offer up information and even advice to the company's clients. They're not out doing the other jobs because they're doing what they do best and enjoy the most."

"You're talking about people specializing a bit more?"

"I'm talking about putting the right people to work at the jobs they do best," Mr. Frame declared. "It seems to me the height of stupidity and inefficiency that you have twenty people in a real estate office and every one of them is supposed to be good at writing marketing materials and ads, good at interacting with people, good at negotiations, intuitive and imaginative in his and her response to the houses that are for sale at any given time, great with numbers, and on and on. It's nuts! A company could be vastly more efficient if it hired the right people for well-defined, well-paying jobs, all of which, taken together, create a wonderful experience for real estate buyers and sellers."

"I'm with you so far."

"Okay. You've got these two in-office workers. They answer the phones. They field client questions. They give people the help they need when they need it rather than passing questions on to the agent in charge of the clients. They also keep the office running efficiently, handling the marketing, following the closing process in close coordination with the title people and others. They are, in many respects, kind of the guts of the operation."

"And?"

"And then you have two or three people whose sole job is to know the current inventory—all the homes for sale and all the homes that have sold within the past year—extremely well. We'll call these people the market researchers. They love what they do. They've seen every relevant house at least once. They've kept very detailed notes on those houses. They get very excited about good properties. They can do two things impeccably. They can tell someone who is going on a listing appointment exactly what the comps are—what houses sold when, who owned them, what motivated the sellers to sell, what amenities and improvements had been added to the homes, what problems existed for the homes, if any—the whole nine yards. And they can listen—and they're good, deep listeners—to the needs and wishes of

John and Suzie Doe, some buyers, and boom, they can instantly rattle off five houses that these buyers really have to see."

"Boom," I repeated.

"And you've got a few people who specialize in listing and marketing properties. They work with the market researchers to develop flawless comparable market analyses to present to potential sellers, and then they go out together with the office marketing manager and give those sellers a presentation that knocks their socks off, makes them laugh, makes them understand the market, and gets their names signed on the listing every time."

"Fun, but I'm beginning to worry about something."

"A three-letter word, right?" Eldred Frame asked.

"Ego," I said. "I guess I'd worry about fear, too. People have tremendous ego attachment to all they do in this business. They want to be responsible for all that goes right, and they want to be able, insofar as it's possible, to sweep their mistakes under the carpet where no one will see them. Furthermore, they want the big prize. They don't want to share the commission with other people. They want that feeling of winning the lottery whenever their hard work leads to the completion of a sale."

"Which is why not everyone would want to work in such a company—just like there are still a lot of people who would rather drink good old Brand X coffee, the one that goes 'beedle-beedle-boop-boop' in the percolator, instead of a latté. But the fact is that everyone in this company is working in the area where he or she is best. Everyone loves what they do. And everyone has constant employment, and is paid very well, including the so-called office staff."

"That's attractive."

"And many people would definitely be attracted to it, especially those who love innovation and professionalism—but that's my own bias showing."

"Any other players?"

"Oh, of course! We haven't mentioned the people who work directly with the buyers. As I said, they coordinate with the market researchers to find the houses their clients should see. They coordinate with an on-site or off-site real estate attorney on all legal matters. All purchase and sale transactions, by the way, are reviewed by this very simpatico attorney, who is also there to answer all the questions that arise. And there's a tax expert on retainer who is there for all the questions that come up."

"Sounds expensive."

"And yes, it is. But no more expensive than what people pay today. I haven't figured out the likely fees—we'd charge fees, not percentage commissions…they're on the way out, no matter what I do, anyway. But the expense of the real estate transaction would be fully justified by the value we've added to every step of the deal."

Eldred Frame paused for a moment, relishing his vision. "Got it all?"

"Mostly," I said. "Are you ever going to get to the part about adventure?"

He laughed. "If we look at a real estate transaction through the eyes of the people who are doing the buying and selling, we see a very fearful thing. How can we transform it all into an adventure that everyone in the family enjoys, understands, and is excited by?"

"I'm not sure," I admitted.

"I don't think there's any one simple answer to that question. It's got to be a whole bunch of things," he said. "Putting people through a multi-media presentation at the outset of buying a home so that the market research guys know, right down to colors and styles, what makes the lights start shining in their eyes. Stopping for ice cream at a certain point, keeping the kids entertained. Having a constant educational system going—with facts about the area, the particular neighborhoods you visit, the current market, etc., always flowing. And, as I said, making the listing presentation into a big, fun deal. Those things are a start."

"My mind is running with all of that."

"That's the thing, Bill. Once you take on a new perspective—once you wonder, for example, what could we create that would both entertain and inform our clients every step of the way?—once you do that, the ideas start to flow."

He smiled. "The bottom line, though," he warned, "is very simple. You want to add value to all that has been done by real estate companies traditionally; you want to simply eliminate the things that companies don't need to do or to lose money on; and you want to provide a new experience for people at a cost that is either smaller or comparable to what they've been used to paying. Then—there you are, steaming off in your very own boat in your very own 'blue ocean,' doing a new kind of real estate that revolutionizes the entire business."

I was a bit stunned by all this. "It's a lot to think about," I admitted.

"See, you were the guy I wanted to try these ideas out on. I wanted to see how you'd react."

"I'm thinking that you haven't negated anything I said in the book," I suggested.

"You're right...though I think it takes a number of things a few steps forward. But you'd still have those office people overseeing the marketing, and you'd rely on informational newsletters and what you call 'free samples' of the services you offer. Again, that's why I came all the way here for this conversation."

So, many months later, we're still talking, Eldred Frame and I.

But as you doubtless already know, Mr. Frame exists only in my imagination, where he challenges me, nags me, suggests wildly new ideas to me, and often won't let me sleep if I wake up in conversation with him in the middle of the night. He can, of course, exist in your imagination now, too. It's a dubious honor, considering what an annoyance he can be, shaking up your peace with his insistent questions and ideas. But he's a great help, it turns out. Given the speed of change in our industry, in the economy, in all aspects of the world in which we live, it can be extremely beneficial to have an outside-the-box, mildly crazed internal voice making sure we're always looking at possible marketing innovations and how we can make the right choices, the ones that clearly reflect who we are.

So I leave Mr. Frame with you, a gift of sorts. May he inspire helpful thoughts and brave innovation in all you do. May he direct you toward the kind of career that supports every aspect of your life. May he help keep you very much alive.

I'd love to hear about your thoughts and experiences and the changes you make. Meantime, may you gather up all the ideas presented in this book, sift through them and find the ones that make the deepest and surest sense to you, mix in elements of who you are, and develop a marketing program that leads inevitably to a deeply satisfying career that is uniquely your own creation.

And I hope to meet you one day and see all that you've done and how well it's worked for you. Perhaps we can talk and laugh about it all while snacking on an exquisite chocolate gelato. Or perhaps I'll show up with a white cane at one of your open houses.

Appendices

APPENDIX ONE

Service-Oriented Marketing Principles

)X(

PRINCIPLE 1   Design All Your Marketing And Prospecting With Your Clients' Needs In Mind. Not Your Own Needs. (Pg. 5)

PRINCIPLE 2   Know Thyself! (Pg. 11)

PRINCIPLE 3   Always Keep The Bigger, Whole-Career Picture In Mind, Not Just Short-Term Concerns. (Pg. 13)

PRINCIPLE 4   A "Warm" Client Is Far More Likely To Result In A Good Transaction, Which Will Bring In Similar "Warm" Clients In The Future. (Pg. 14)

PRINCIPLE 5   Always Expect The Best For Your Clients And From Your Clients, And Also For Yourself And From Yourself. (Pg. 17)

PRINCIPLE 6   You Must Love And Enjoy What You Are Doing, And Make Sure You Have Time For All That You Love In Your Life. (Pg. 18)

PRINCIPLE 7   Learn All You Can From Those Among Your Fellow Associates At Work Who Offer Support, Stimulate Your Mind, And Model The Ways Of Doing Business That You Wish To Emulate. (Pg. 22)

PRINCIPLE 8   Do Not Limit Your Friendships To Your Own Office Or Company, And Do Not Let The Misleading Idea That Someone Is Your "Competition" Keep You From Creating Beneficial Relationships With Such People. (Pg. 22)

PRINCIPLE 9   You, As A Real Estate Professional, Are Not The Right Person For Every Potential Client In The Known Universe. (Pg. 24)

PRINCIPLE 10   Though It's Important Never To Stop Marketing Yourself Effectively, It's Also Important To Do So In A Way That Burns Up The Least Amount Of Your Time And Shoe Leather. (Pg. 29)

PRINCIPLE 11   You Need To Design A Marketing Program That You Can Keep Going Even When You Get Very, Very Busy With Clients. (Pg. 30)

APPENDIX TWO

Acknowledgements

First and foremost, my editor, my formatter, my cheerleader, best friend and lifemate, Robyn, has been essential to the fact that all of this information was collected into a book. She has a long history with my writings, longer even than our marriage, and she has talked with our newsletter clients for years, gaining a good feeling for the marketing programs that truly do work. It's largely because of her help and support that everything packed into this book, based on years of experience, does work.

Equally important in the great scheme of things are my dear colleagues, Rand and Jill Fleischman, who have helped to turn this career of mine into a thrilling adventure. Who could imagine business colleagues becoming such dear friends? I am blessed by their support, questions, curiosity, ideas and kindness every day and, though it is probably a cliché, this book indeed would not exist without their invaluable help.

Huge gratitude goes out to Joan Machlis, who offered (without being asked) to pick up her fine-tooth comb and go through every word of this book, both for clarity and for typos. She has also provided mountains of encouragement. Thanks, too, to Jenny "Hawkeye" Craun and Tamara LaChimia for their proofing and great insights.

And to my dear friends, the Rev. Jim Friedrich and (Soon-to-be-Rev.) Karen Haig, who listened as I read my book and clarified the title it wanted. It makes my book feel specially blessed somehow.

I must add thanks to my student and friend, Caleb Schmidt, who designed the original cover for the book, giving me the thrill of coming that much closer to a finished piece of work. And a client and instant friend, Jake Hesseltine (Jake.Hesseltine@gmail.com), who took the photo for the back cover one windy day in Old Town, San Diego. Jake is a mortgage professional and a superb photographer, a Jack of Two Trades, master of both. He knows what it means to follow his passion.

I need, too, to heap praise and gratitude on the amazing Tricia Kelly (tricia@e-dezin.com), who created the final covers and formatted the inside of this book. She approached the task with great and tender care, even as her life was convulsed by personal earthquakes, and dazzled me with the outcome.

From here, I could thank my father and mother and sister and brother and all of Rabbit's Friends and Relations (as in *Winnie the Pooh*) but I will simply remember a man who looked at all my work with great critical wisdom—he was my own Eldred Frame, cranky, honest, probing, loving...my grandfather, Ira N. Frisbee. I hope they've had the wisdom to put him in charge of all the number-crunching in the Great Accounting House out there in the Great Beyond. He loved to do it, advising me hundreds of times, "Bill, there is nothing so satisfying as good, hard work." I didn't want to hear that when I was a teenager, but I think of it fondly and often these days...usually when I've finished the work at hand and am ready for a great cup of gelato.

APPENDIX THREE
Who Is Bill Fisher, Ph.D.?

Bill Fisher dove into real estate in 1976, quickly becoming one of the most successful real estate professionals in Orange County, building his business with a combination of newsletters sent regularly to his target market, community events he produced, and the kind of knowledgeable, caring service that created great word-of-mouth advertising.

Soon other real estate professionals asked him to create newsletters for them as well, and a second business began to develop. Bill had learned a great deal about research and writing in the graduate work that led to a Masters and Ph.D. degree in English literature. He's also a lifelong student of marketing, partly because of the mentorship of remarkable men like Joe Coulombe, who developed Trader Joe's Markets. The marketing materials Bill has produced for the last quarter of a century and more—for real estate and mortgage professionals and for title insurance companies throughout the United States—have consistently been called the best in the business, and many of his clients have been relying on his services for twenty years and more.

Though his research and writing schedule is always very full, Bill finds time to write poetry, songs, and stories, as well as essays on economic issues. He loves to teach as well, and devotes at least one month a year to working with students on their own writing abilities. Over the years, he has developed and taught courses in real estate financing, and spoken on various aspects of the real estate market.

After having lived most of his life in Southern California, Bill now lives in the Pacific Northwest with his wife, a greatly-respected high school teacher—with whom he has recorded two CDs of their own music, and with whom he performs at local music festivals and coffee houses. His three stepchildren are similarly passionate about music and the arts, and excel at keeping Bill young at heart and very alive in mind.

You can communicate with Bill at wedwrap@comcast.net.

APPENDIX FOUR
More Info And Assistance

For Further Samples of Newsletters and
Information on Service-Oriented Marketing...

You can see samples of the newsletters created each month,
along with a full explanation of how our service works—
including a mailing service that makes sure your materials
are sent each month to your target market—by visiting...

www.rightsidemarketing.com.

You can also get any further questions answered,
and talk about your own marketing program, by calling
the great people at Right Side Marketing...

800.456.4395.

And order more copies of this book at...

www.Trafford.com/06-2862.

Dr. Bill Fisher is available at...
wedwrap@comcast.net.

And visit his blog at *youarenotahouse.blogspot.com*

Bill writes several personalized prospecting newsletters, all customizable, each month for the clients of Right Side Marketing. He
and his colleagues Rand and Jill Fleischman also send out a monthly
newsletter, *The Right Times*, to clients. Often humorous, always up-to-
the-minute, this letter suggests new approaches to Service-Oriented
Marketing.

We welcome your thoughts, inquiries, suggestions, and any other
feedback.